AF521835

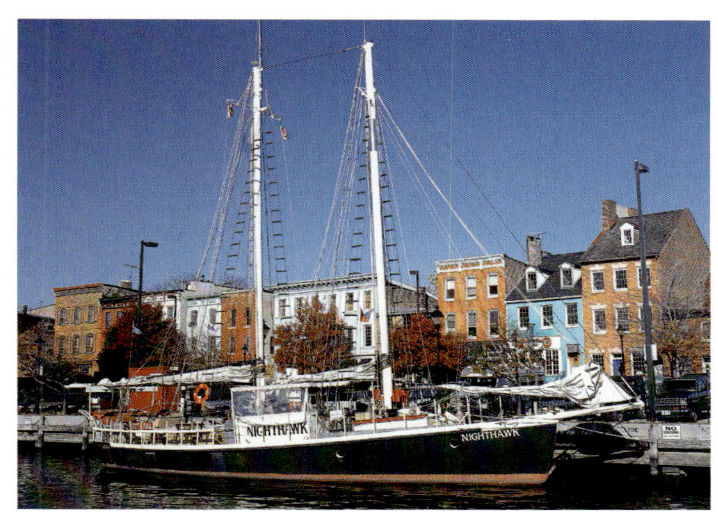
NIGHTHAWK
NIGHTHAWK

MARYLAND

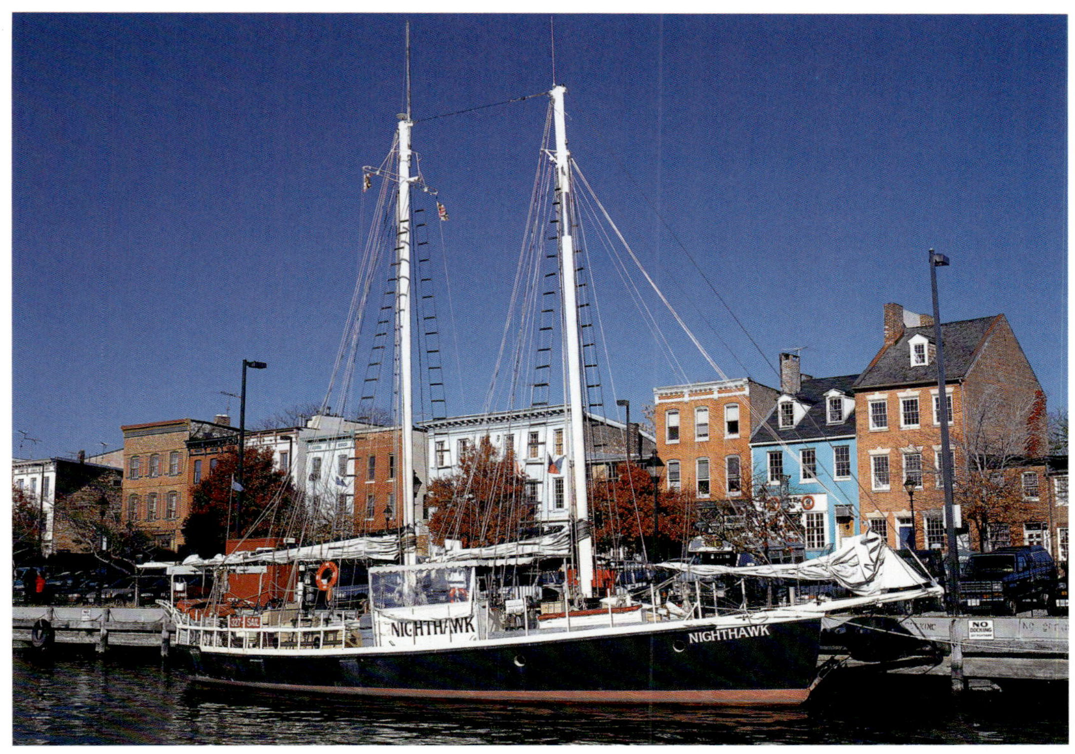

WHITECAP BOOKS

Text by Tanya Lloyd Kyi
Edited by Elaine Jones
Photo editing by Tanya Lloyd Kyi
Proofread by Lisa Collins
Cover and interior layout by Jacqui Thomas

Printed and bound in Canada

National Library of Canada Cataloguing in Publication Data

Kyi, Tanya Lloyd, 1973–
Maryland

(America series)
ISBN 1-55285-417-5

1. Maryland—Pictorial works. I. Title. II. Series: Kyi, Tanya Lloyd, 1973— America series.
F182.K94 2003 975.2'044'0222 C2002-911391-1

The publisher acknowledges the support of the Canada Council and the Cultural Services Branch of the Government of British Columbia in making this publication possible. We acknowledge the financial support of the Government of Canada through the Book Publishing Industry Development Program for our publishing activities.

Skipjacks, Maryland's oyster boats of the past, bob on the waves of Chesapeake Bay. Charter vessels dock and fishers disembark, proudly displaying the day's catch. Seafood eateries and local brew pubs open their doors and the clinking of glasses and the chatter of guests floats from the patios over the calm waters.

The shoreline of Chesapeake Bay traces the history of this region. To geologists, it tells of the ice age 10,000 years ago, when melting glaciers formed the waterway. To archeologists, the pottery and burial sites here hint at the long-ago lives of the Conoy, Patuxent, Choptank, and Assateague peoples. To historians, the shoreline conjures the voyage of Captain John Smith. When he sailed the bay in 1608, he described the region as rich in a bounty of seafood, girded by fertile farmland.

Just as the waters supported a host of sea life, they offered sustenance to the colonists who settled here almost four centuries ago. When the villages on the shores became successful, settlers moved slowly inland, discovering the Appalachian foothills of Maryland's western frontier, tracing the path of the Potomac River, and farming the abundant valleys.

Sightseers today discover all this and more, traveling from the forests of Catoctin Mountain Park and the sites of the Chesapeake and Ohio Canal National Historic Park to the bustling harbor of Baltimore and the elegant streets of Annapolis. The marinas of St. Michaels and the antique shops of North Beach attract some travelers, while the rock climbing routes of Caderock and the shifting sands of Assateague National Seashore await the more adventurous.

Dotted with lighthouses, stockades, or Civil-War battlefields, each region bears reminders of Maryland's varied past. But the state's residents also know how to enjoy the present. The cheering crowds at a Baltimore Orioles game, the cyclists exploring Rock Creek Park, and the revelers at Ocean City's midway all bear witness to the lively character of Maryland today.

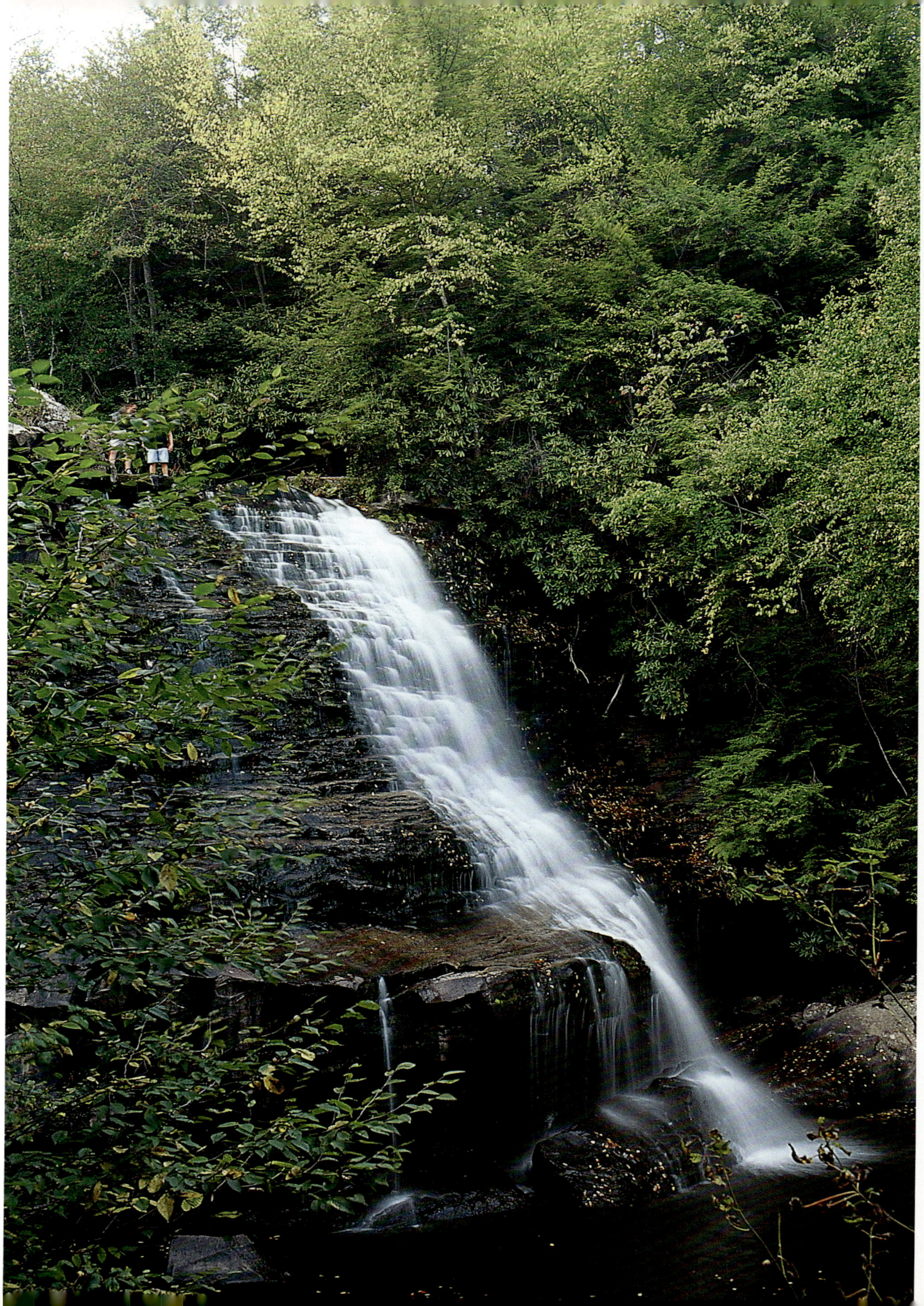

Hiking trails through the old-growth forest of Swallow Falls State Park lead sightseers to the highest free-falling waterfall in the state, 63-foot Muddy Creek Falls. The preserve also offers the rapids and canyons of the Youghiogheny River, which winds along the park borders.

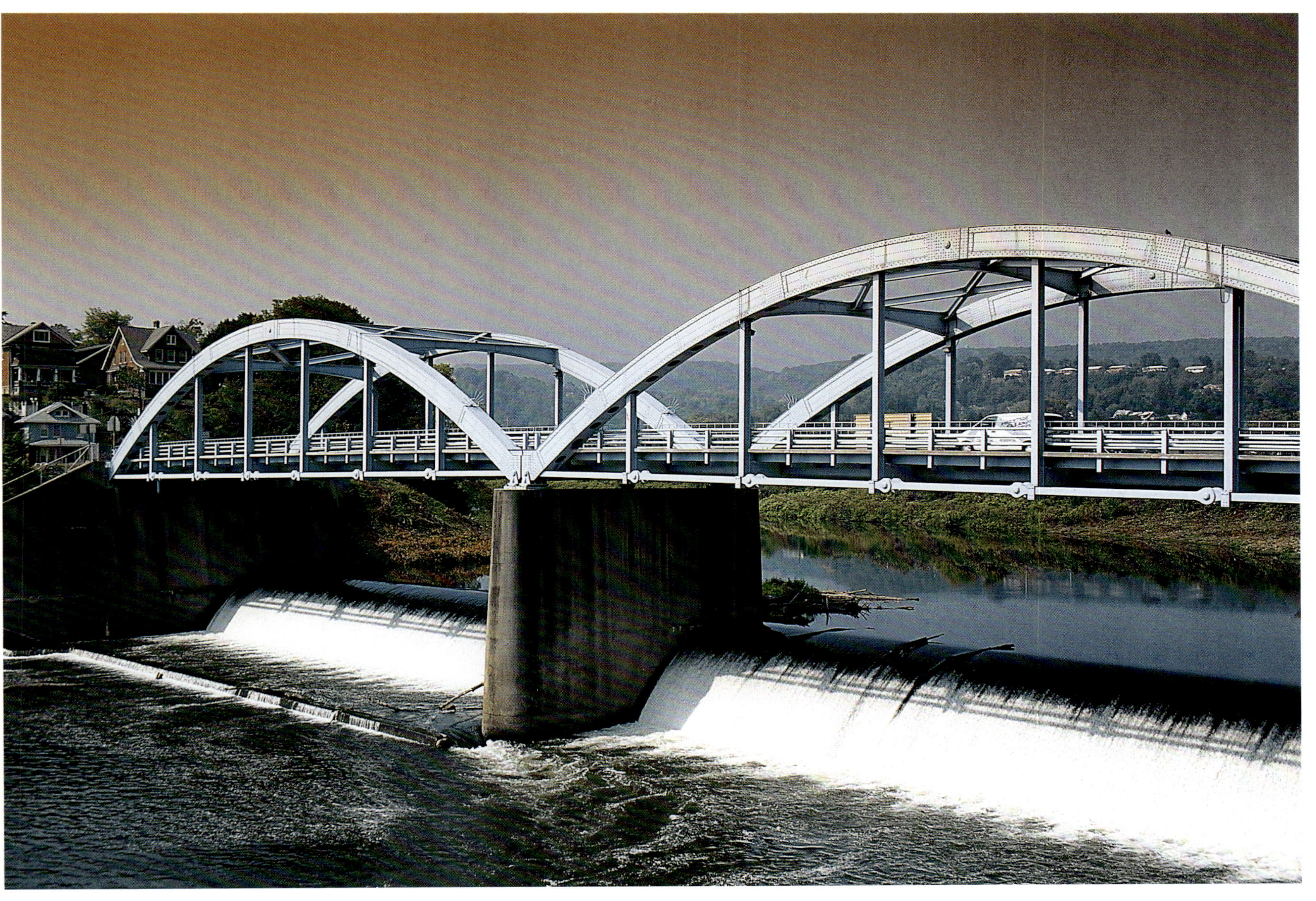

When the Ohio Company's agent, Christopher Gist, traveled western Maryland in 1749, the junction of Wills Creek and the Potomac River's north branch seemed an ideal place for a stockade and trading post. Six years later, General Edward Braddock established Fort Cumberland at the outpost.

Campsites, hiking trails, and an expanse of remote wilderness draw visitors to Deep Creek Lake in western Maryland. The lake was created by a hydroelectric dam built on Deep Creek in the 1920s. Today, the surrounding forest is home to black bears, wild turkeys, bobcats, and whitetail deer.

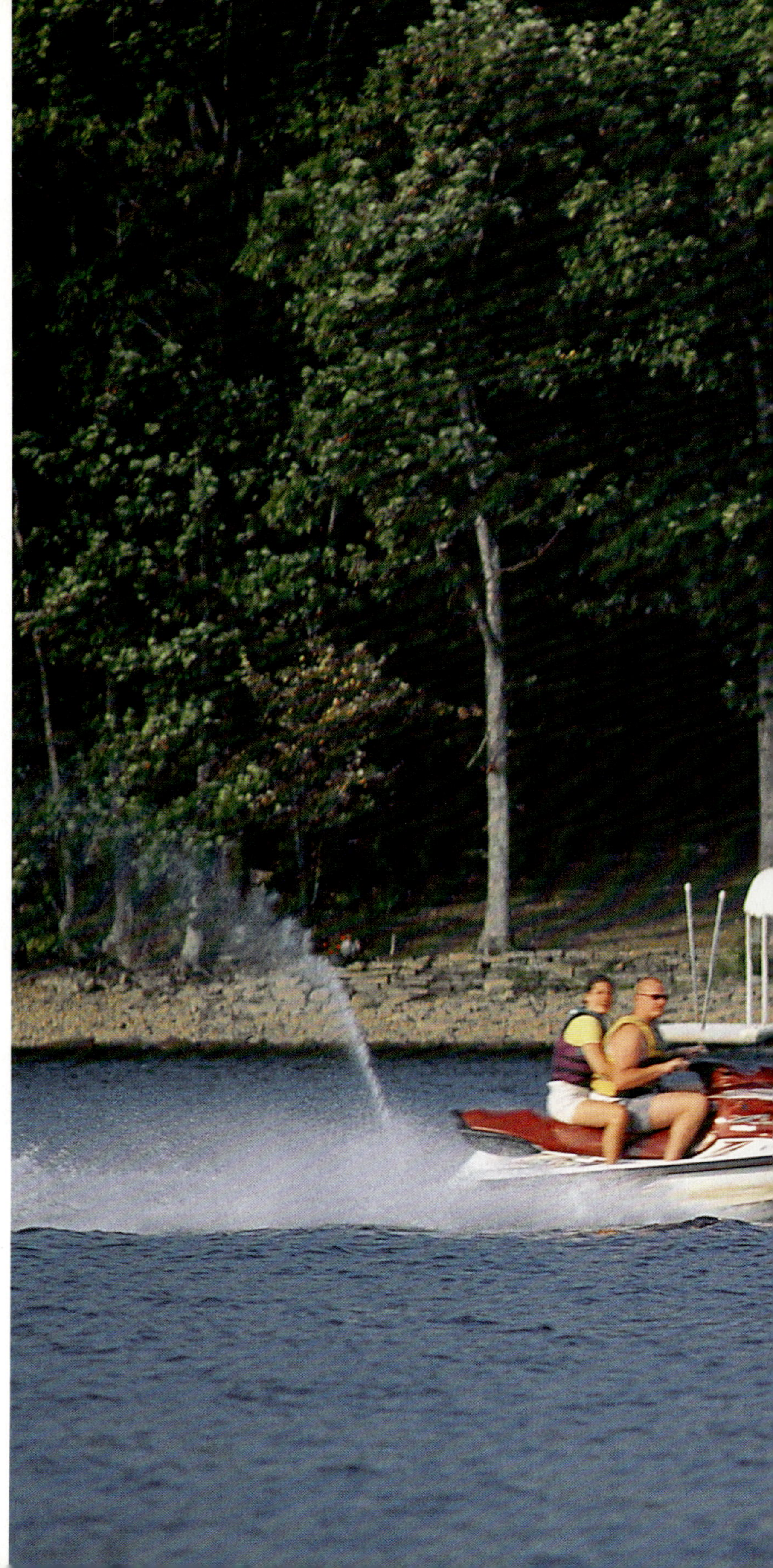

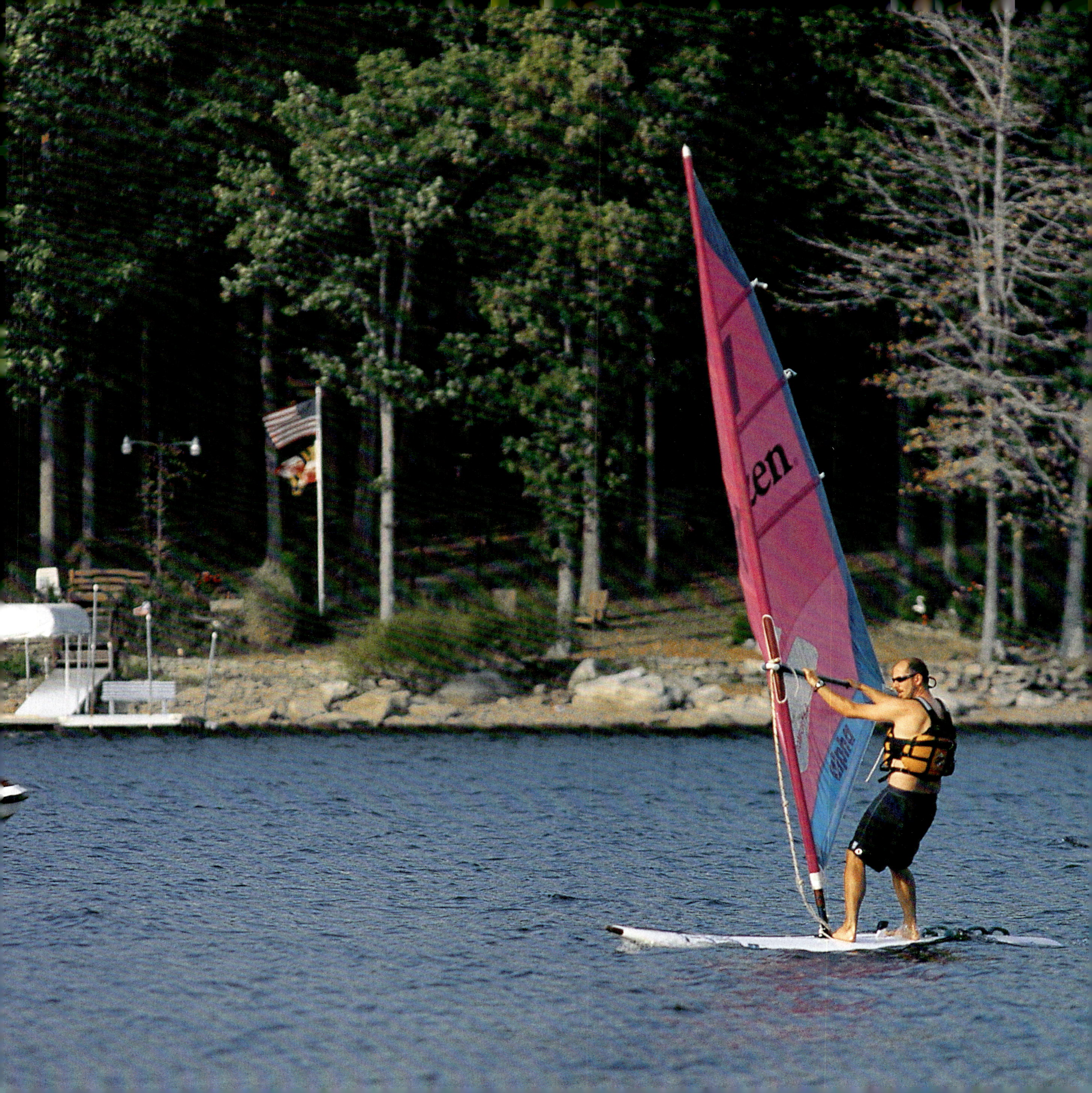

An iron truss bridge, a horseshoe curve, and a 914-foot-long tunnel under Piney Mountain—these are some of the adventures awaiting passengers on the Western Maryland Scenic Railroad. Departing from Cumberland, the railway offers a round trip through some of the state's most scenic land-scapes, including a stop at the restored train depot in Frostburg.

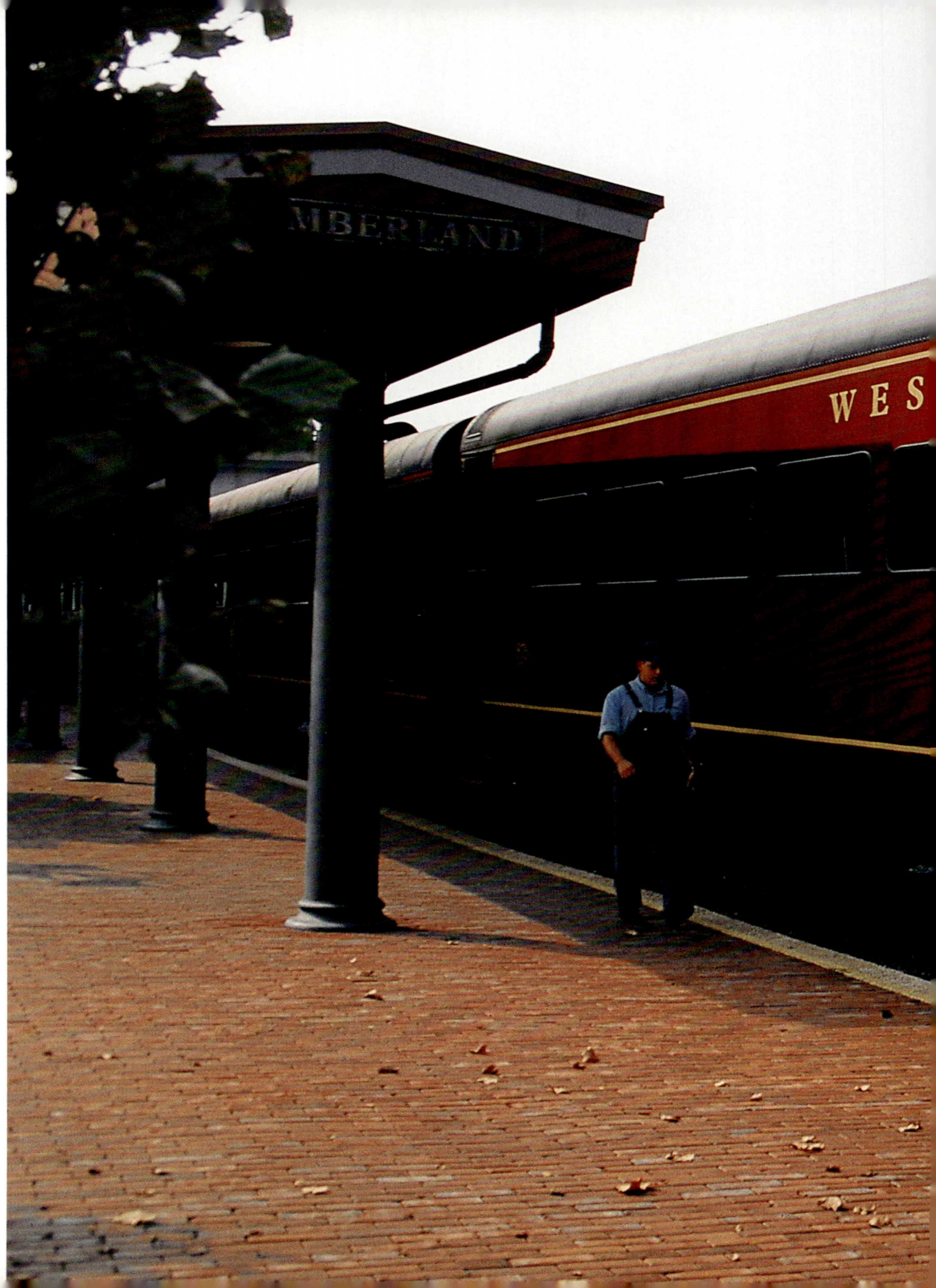

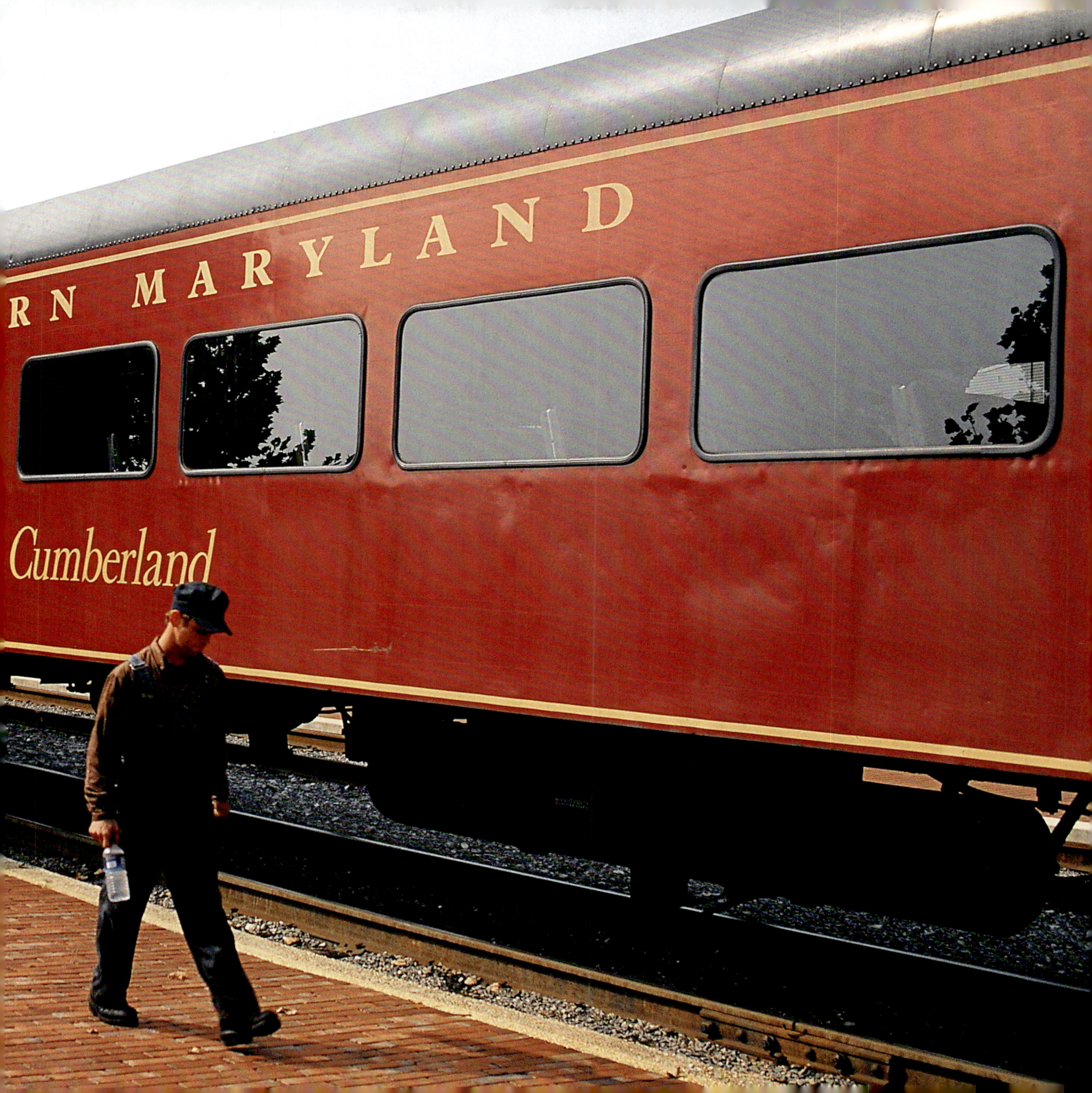
RN MARYLAND
Cumberland

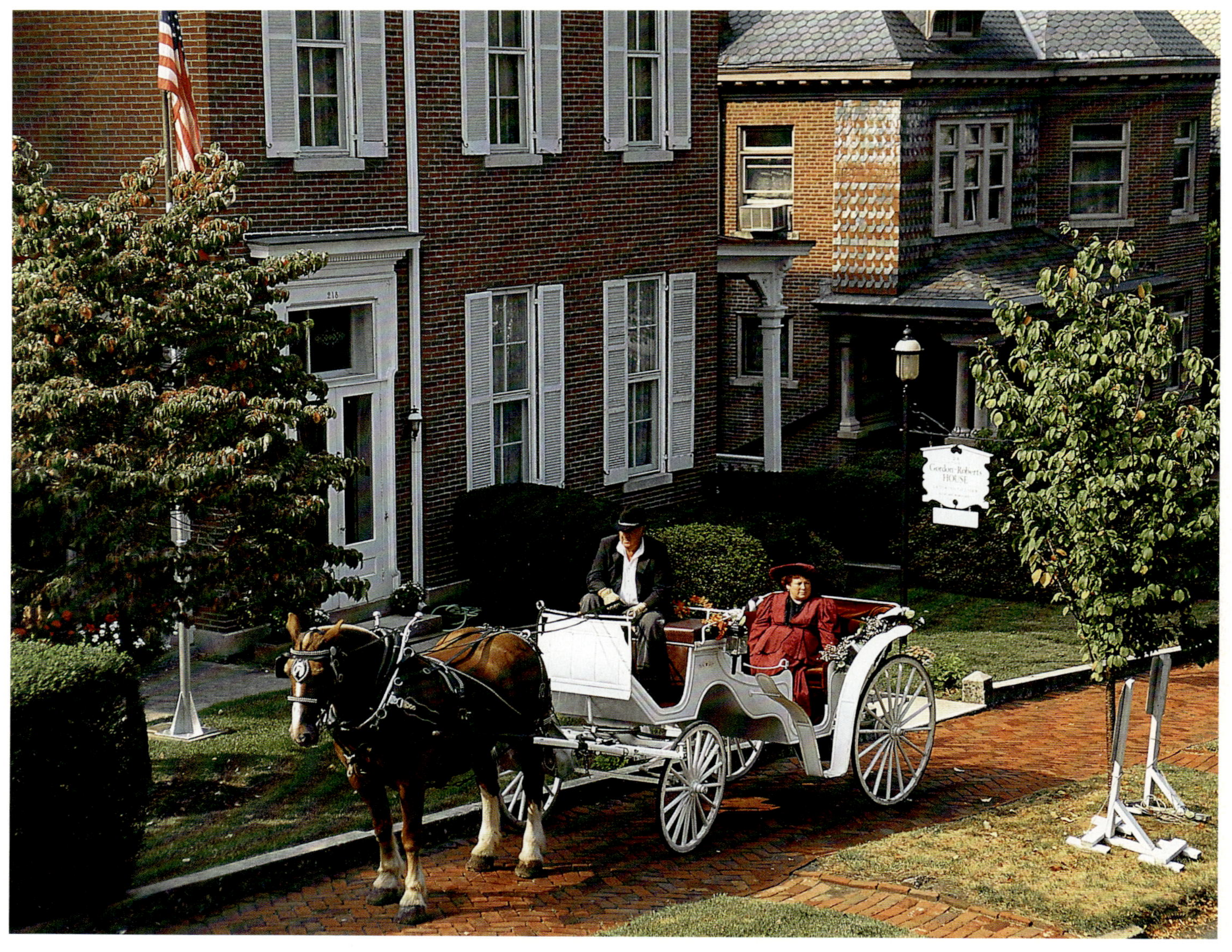

A horse and carriage ride through Cumberland's Historic District gives tourists a look at the Victorian homes built for coal barons and railway builders of the past. The neighborhood's crown jewel is History House. The elegant 18-room mansion was built in 1867 for the president of the Chesapeake and Ohio Canal.

In September 1862, General Robert E. Lee marched his Confederate troops north, hoping to force Abraham Lincoln to sue for peace. His men were not only met by Union troops, they were captured in the bloodiest and most decisive victory of the Civil War. Antietam National Battlefield commemorates the events.

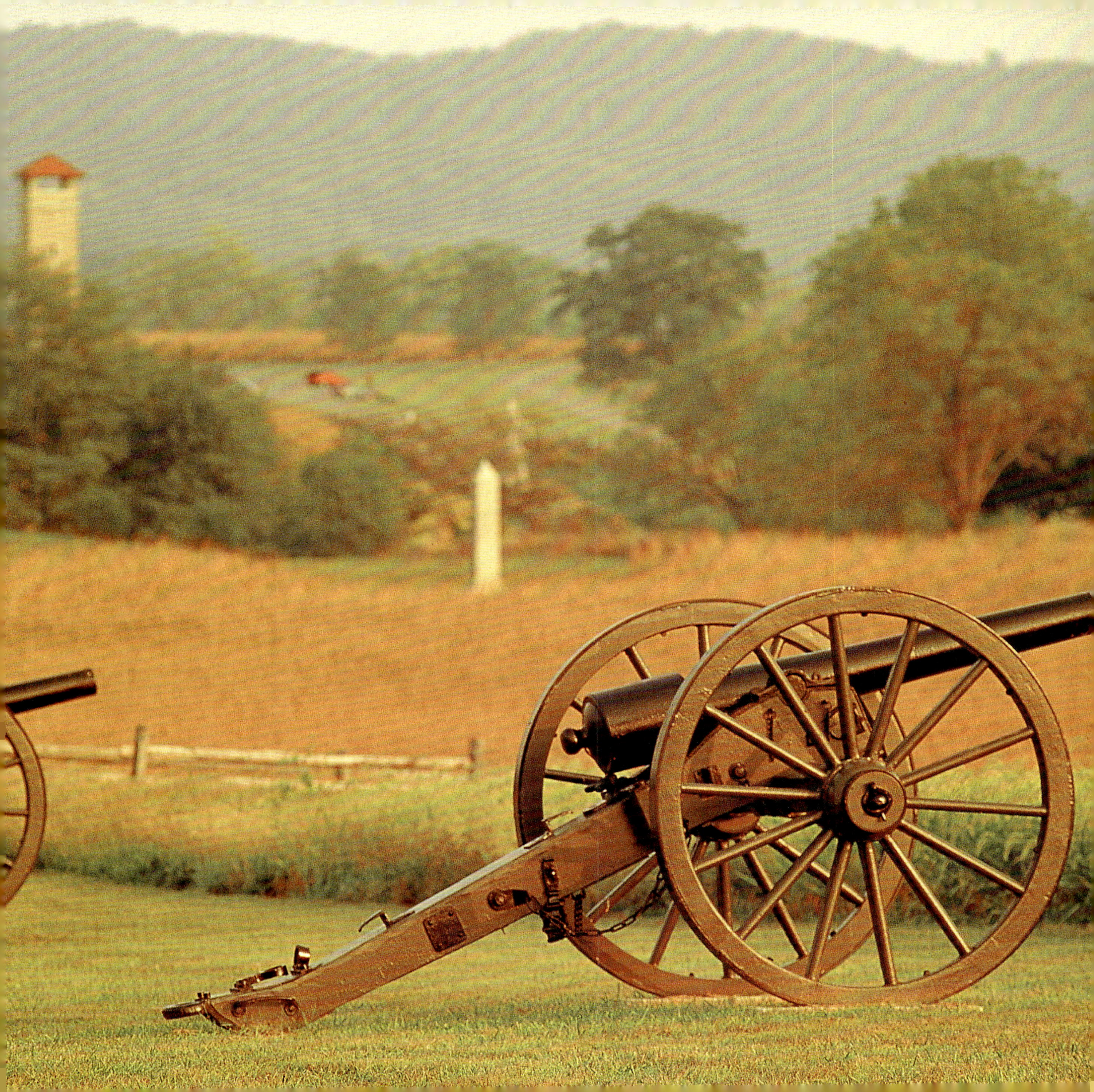

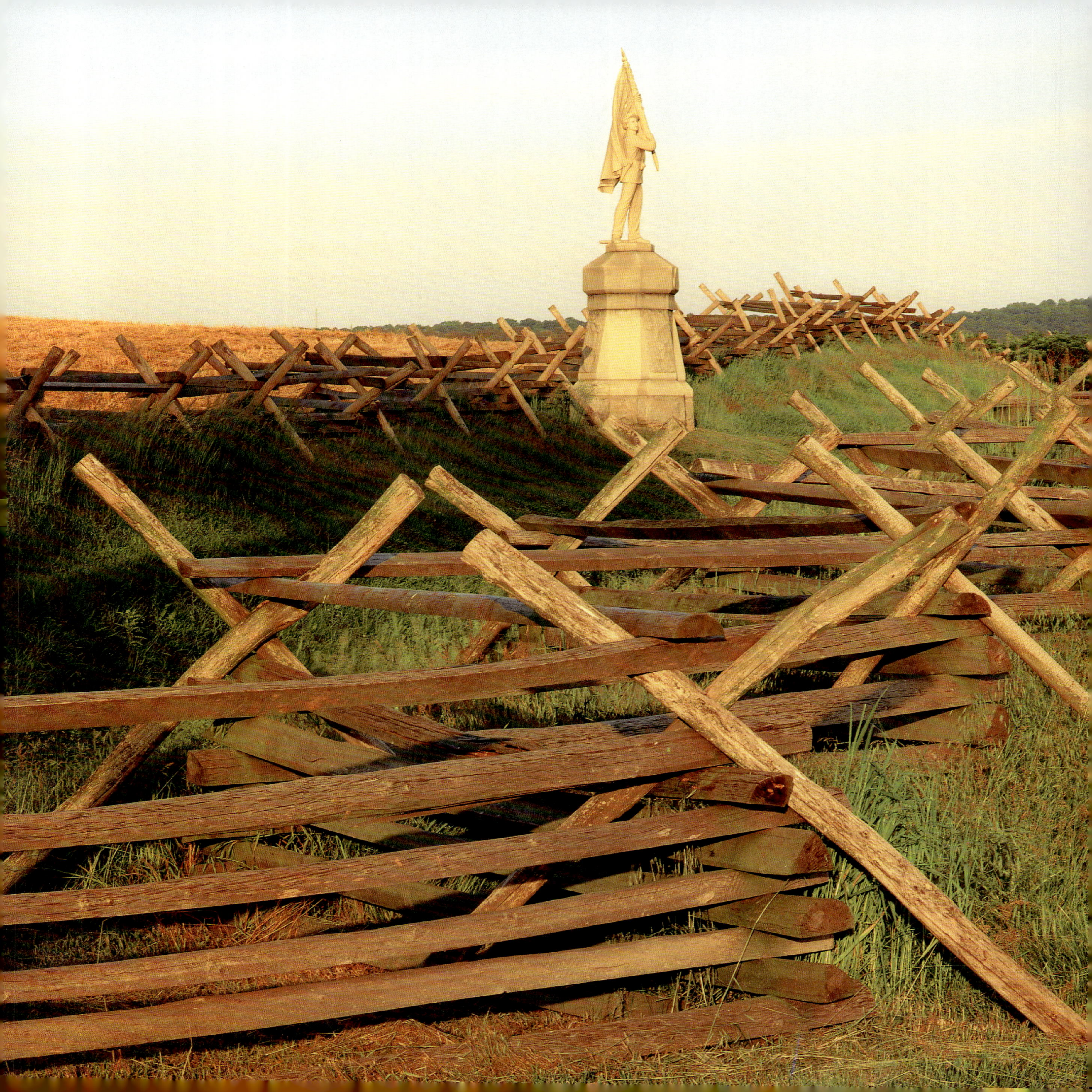

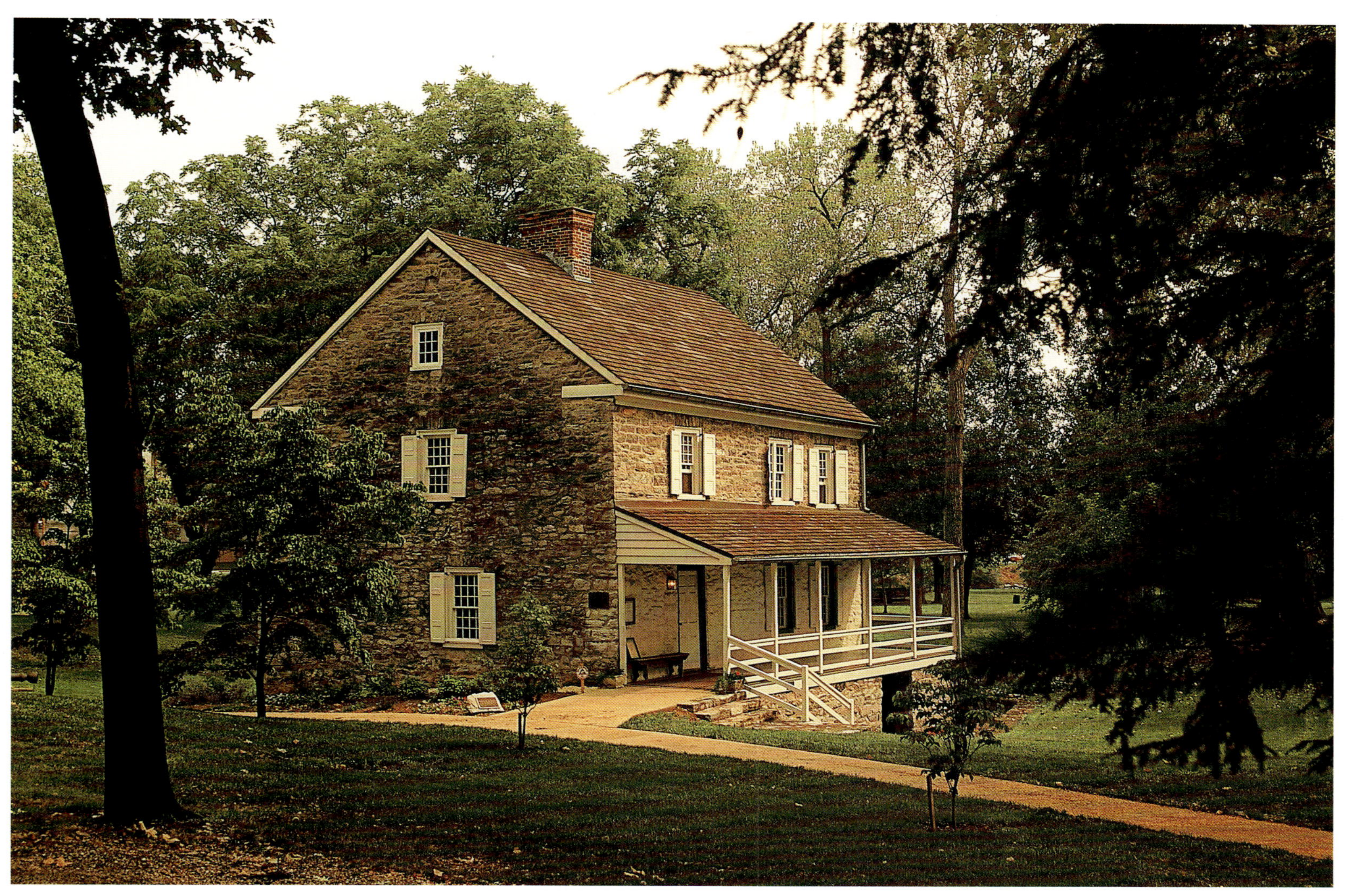

Jonathan Hager, founder of Hagerstown, built this house in 1739. The German immigrant and trader built his home of 22-inch-thick stone and positioned it over two natural springs, ensuring the structure could serve as a fortification in case of attack. After making his fortune in trade and land speculation, Hager was elected to the General Assembly at Annapolis in 1773.

In the worst clash of the Civil War, 3,650 soldiers were killed and 17,300 were wounded. The Battle of Antietam caused more casualties than the Revolutionary War, the War of 1812, the Mexican War, and the Spanish-American War combined. The Union victory, however, gave Abraham Lincoln the support he needed to declare the abolition of slavery.

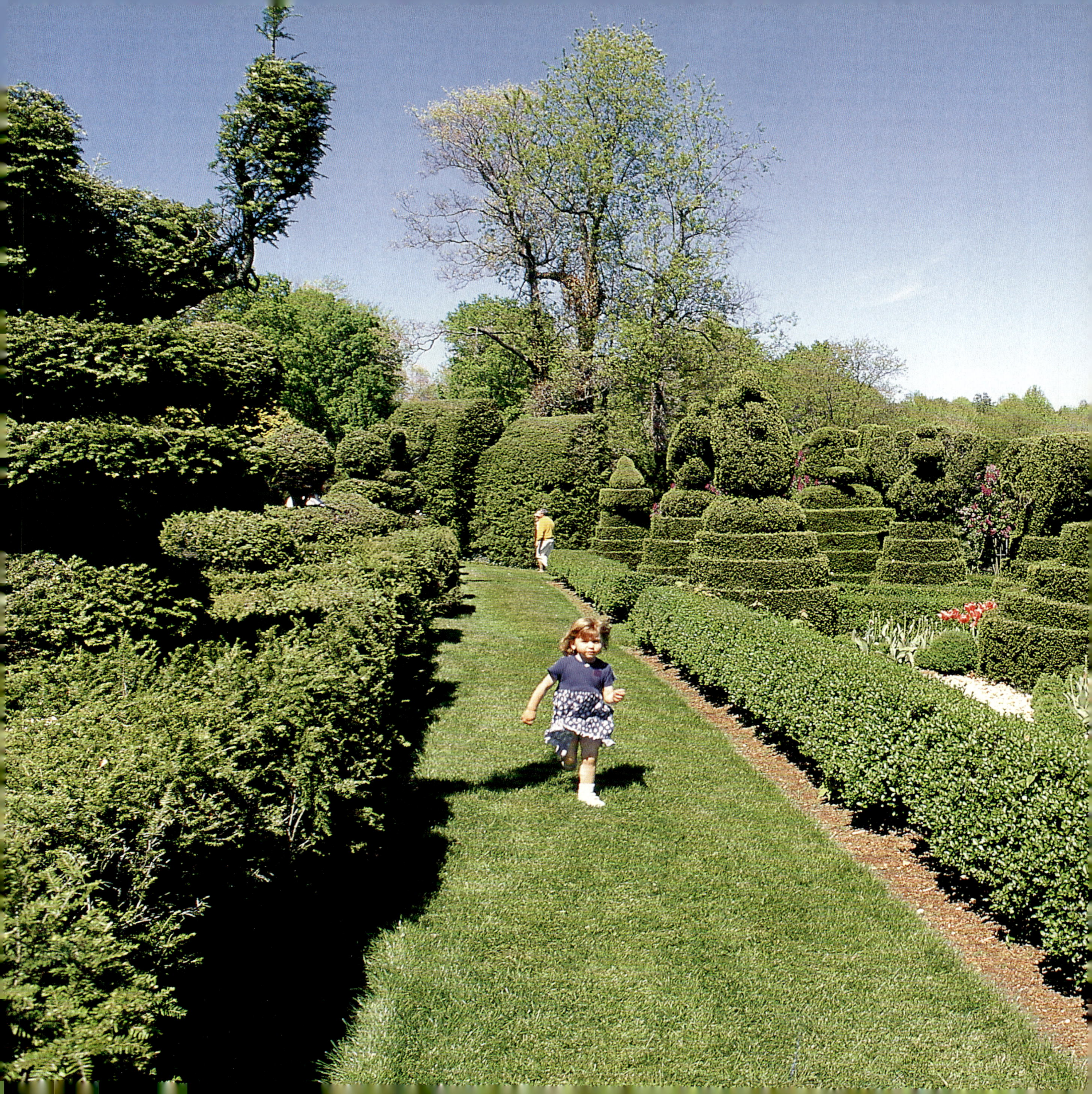

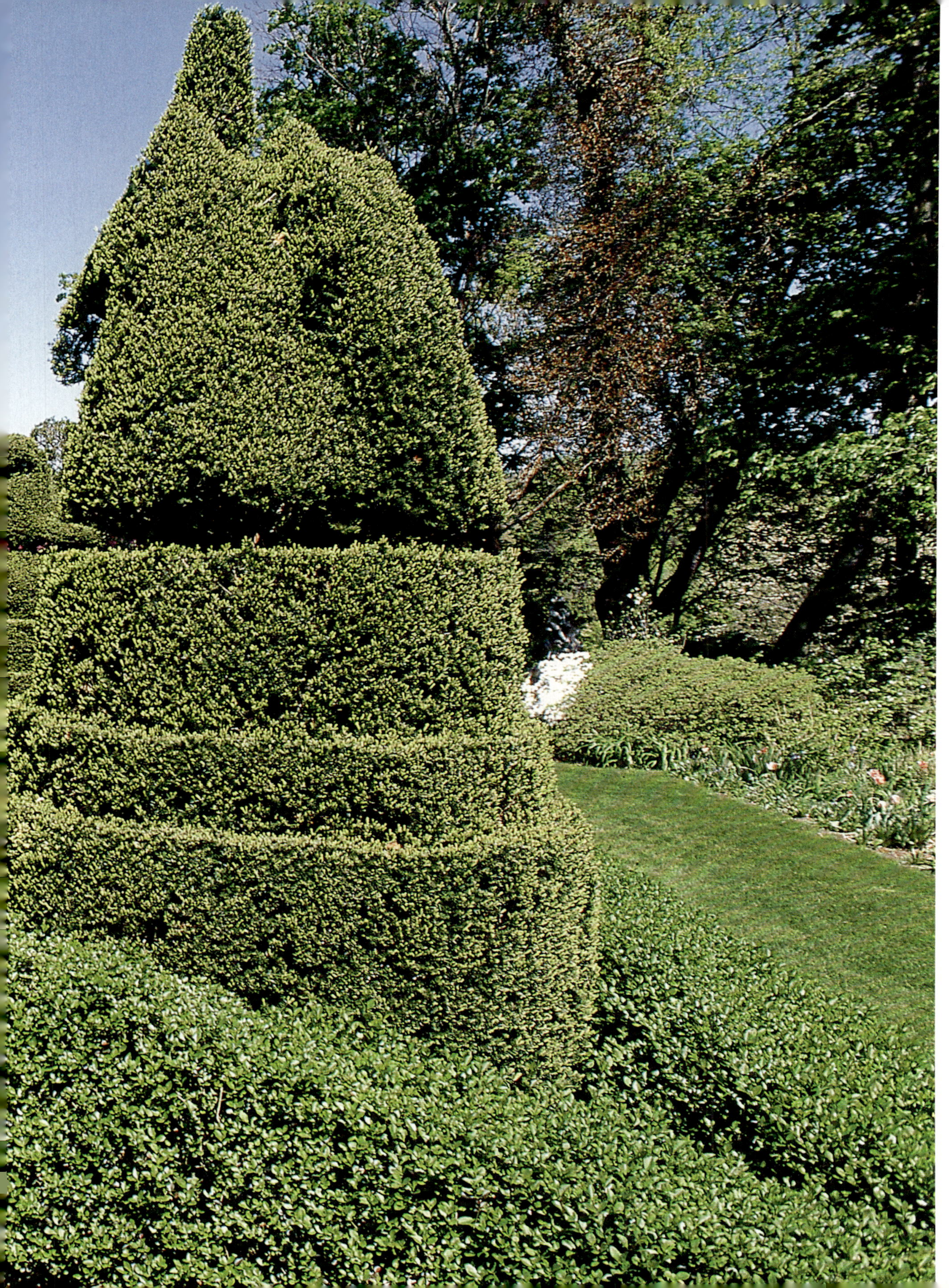

The Garden Club of America has called Ladew Topiary Gardens the most outstanding topiary gardens in the nation. Aristocratic owner Harvey S. Ladew had already spent several years building and fox-hunting on his western Maryland property when he began cultivating the 22-acre garden in the late 1930s. He based several of his 15 themed garden "rooms" on designs he had seen on his European travels.

For Maryland residents, Catoctin Mountain Park is a forest playground, with camping, picnicking, hiking, and fishing facilities. The U.S. president arrives here looking for similar opportunities. Camp David, the presidential retreat, lies nearby, in a portion of the park not open to the public.

Facing Page
In the early 1900s, settlers cleared large sections of land in this western Maryland forest, using the timber to fuel the local iron furnace. In 1954, the state began rehabilitating 5,000 acres—land that became Cunningham Falls State Park. The 78-foot series of cascades awaits visitors down a scenic half-mile hiking trail.

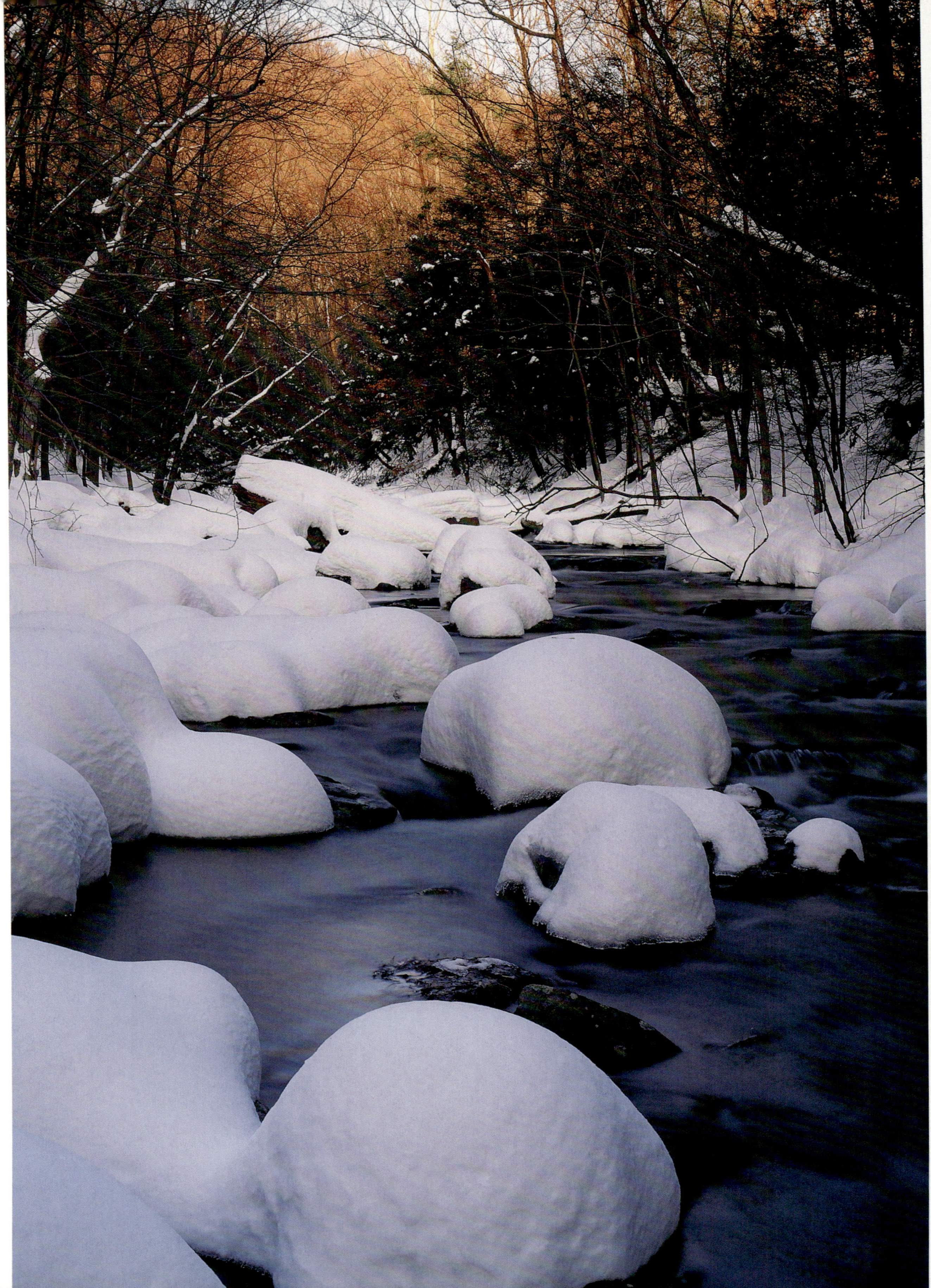

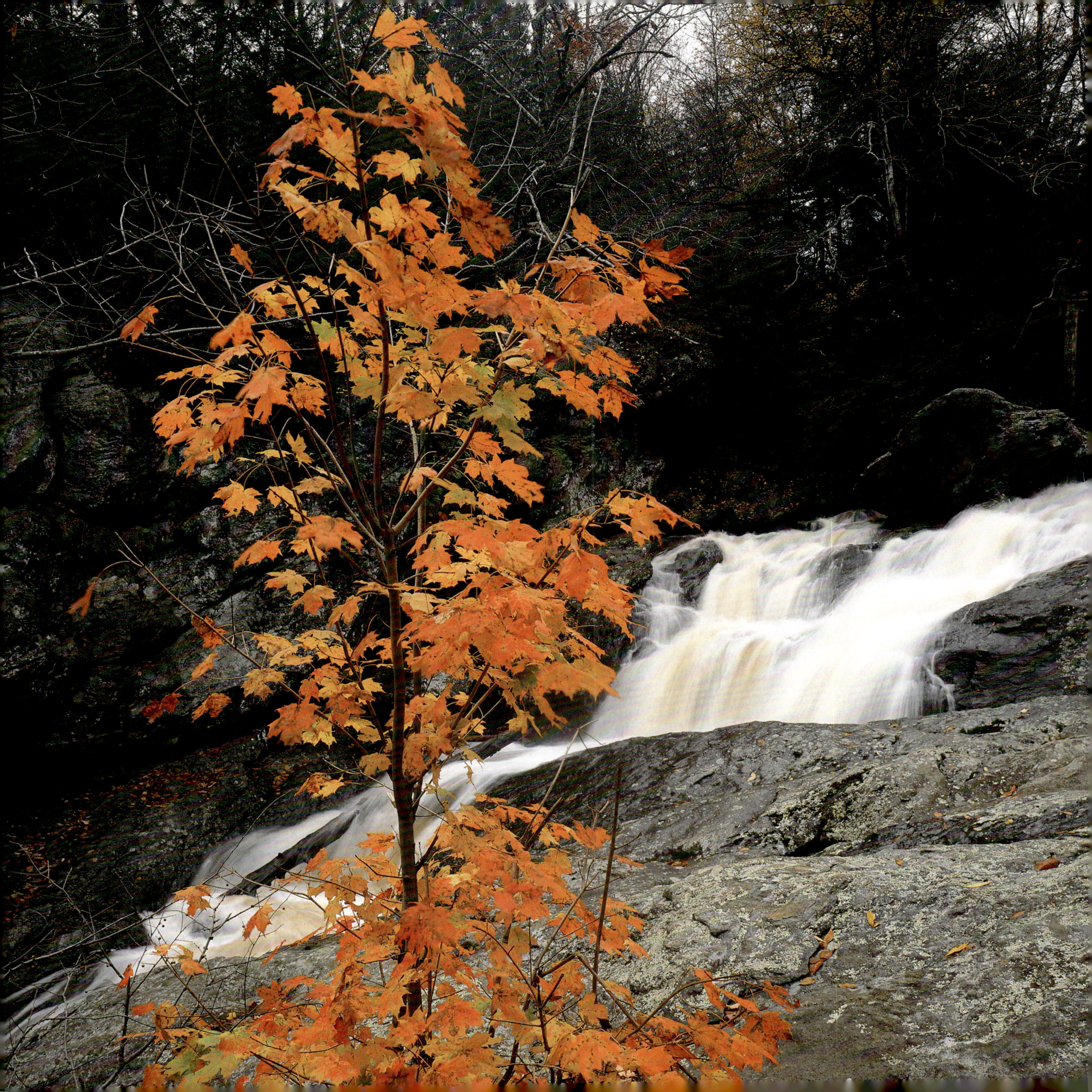

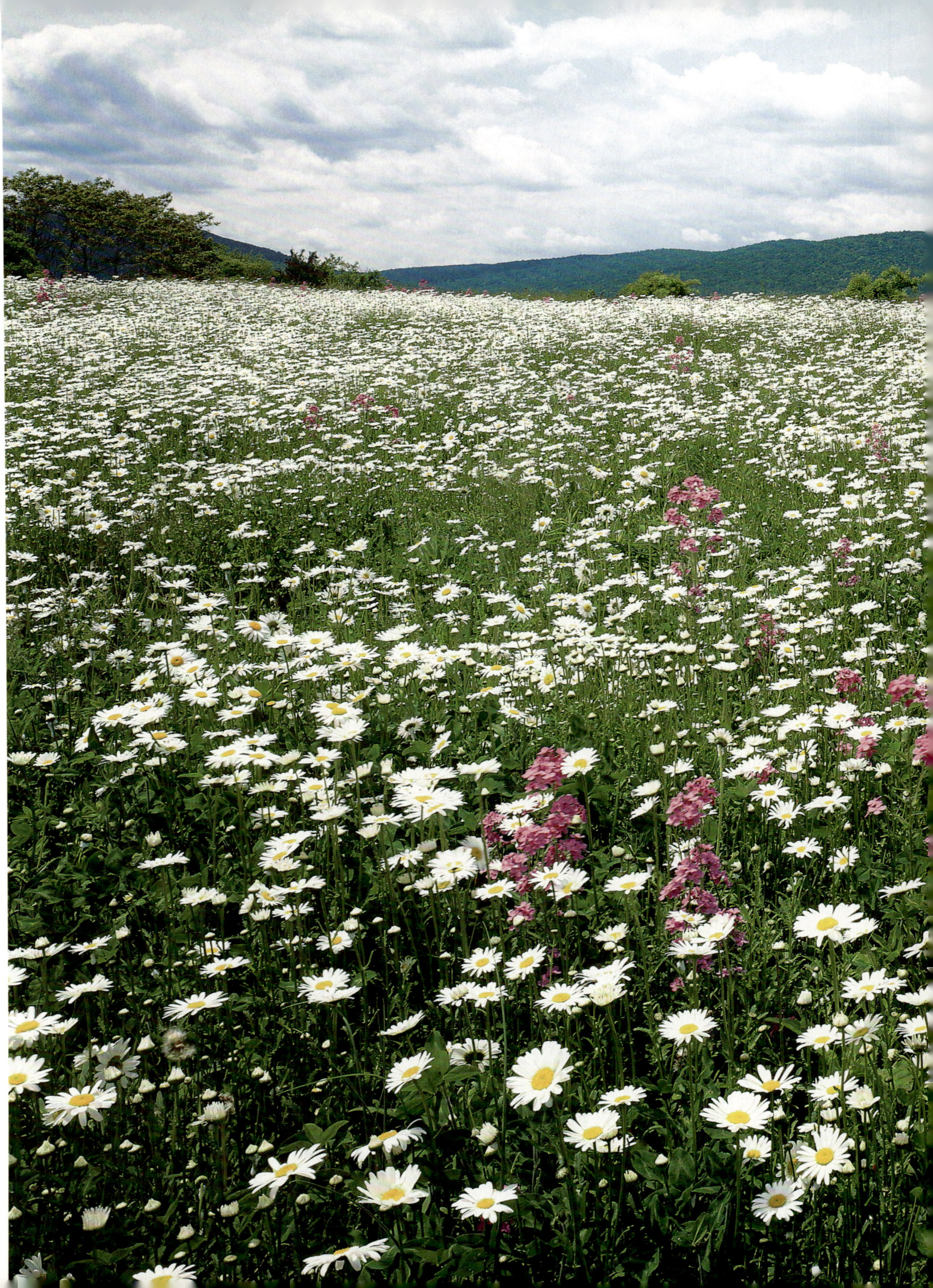

Wildflowers carpet the meadows of the Allegheny foothills in Frederick County. The Allegheny Range lies across Shenandoah Valley from Virginia's famous Blue Ridge Mountains. Together, these series of summits form part of the Appalachian Range, a 1,500-mile-long string of peaks stretching parallel to the Atlantic coast from Alabama to Canada.

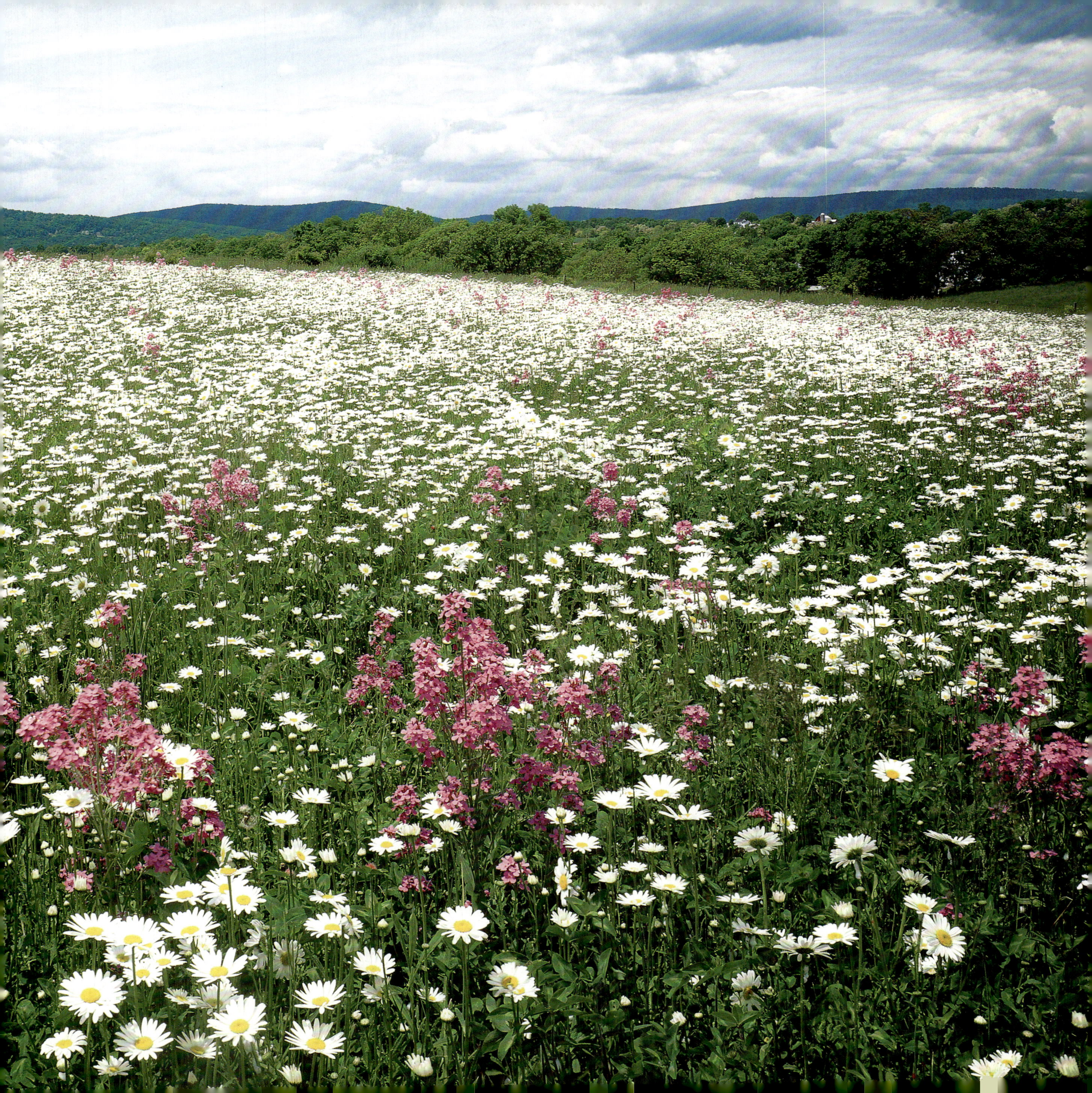

During the Civil War, Frederick served as a supply depot as both Confederate and Union troops moved back and forth through the region. The town was also a strategic location during the Revolutionary War, though no battles were fought here. Francis Scott Key, who wrote America's national anthem, was born in Frederick.

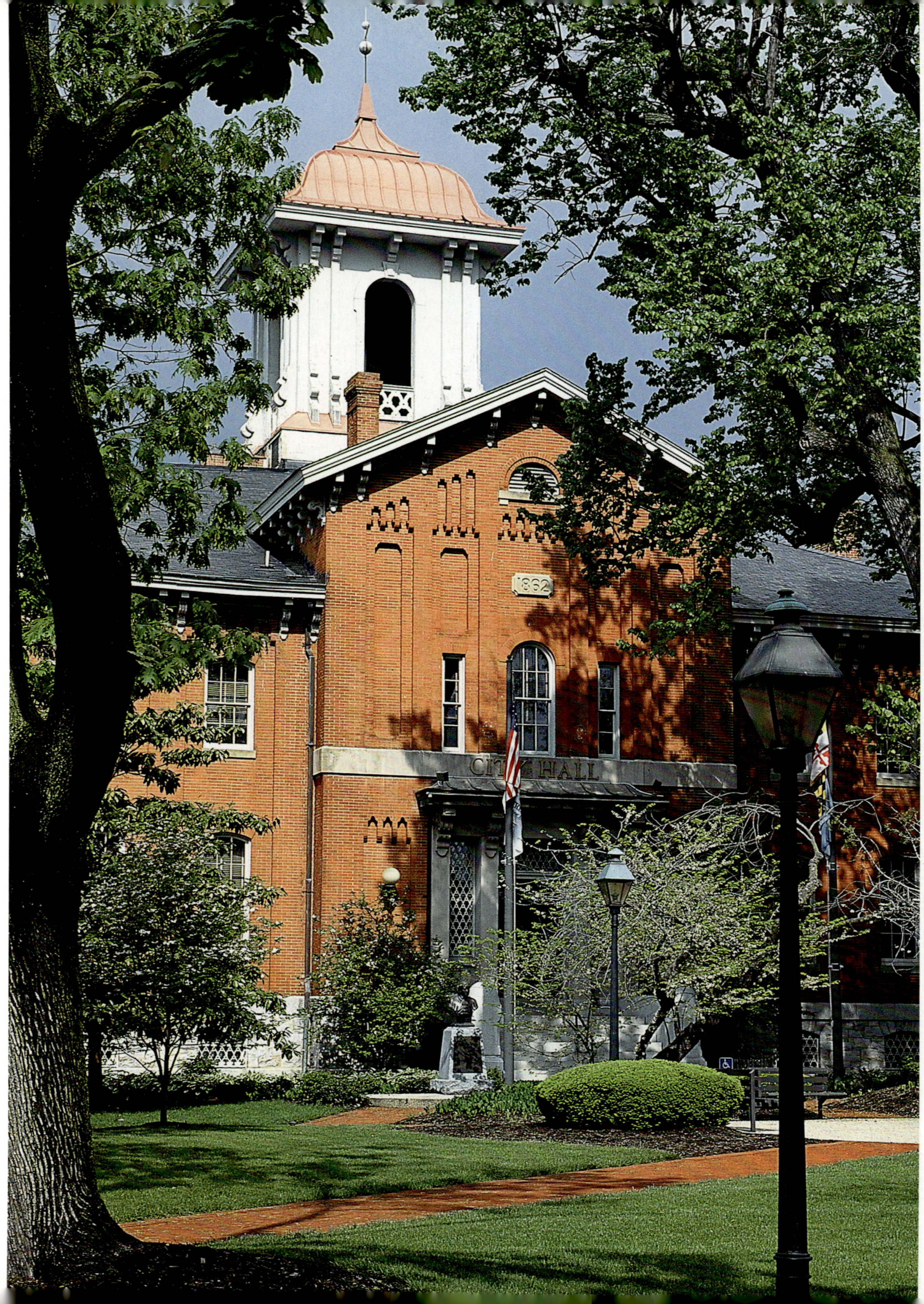

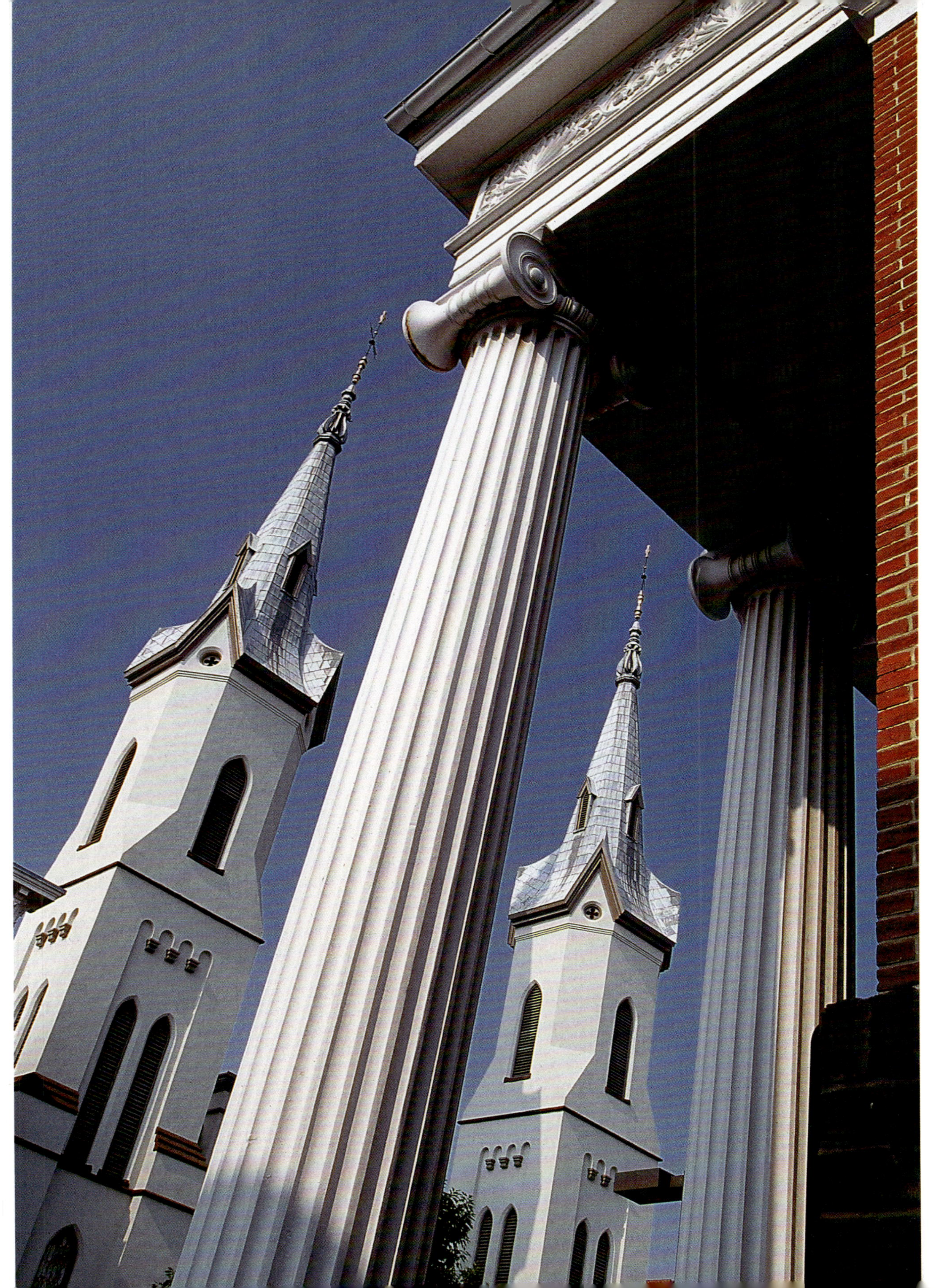

The church spires of Frederick are the most prominent landmarks on the city skyline. The first three churches were established here in the 1740s, when 100 settlers arrived to farm the surrounding land. Though Frederick has grown to become Maryland's second-largest center, the city has protected the views of its famous spires.

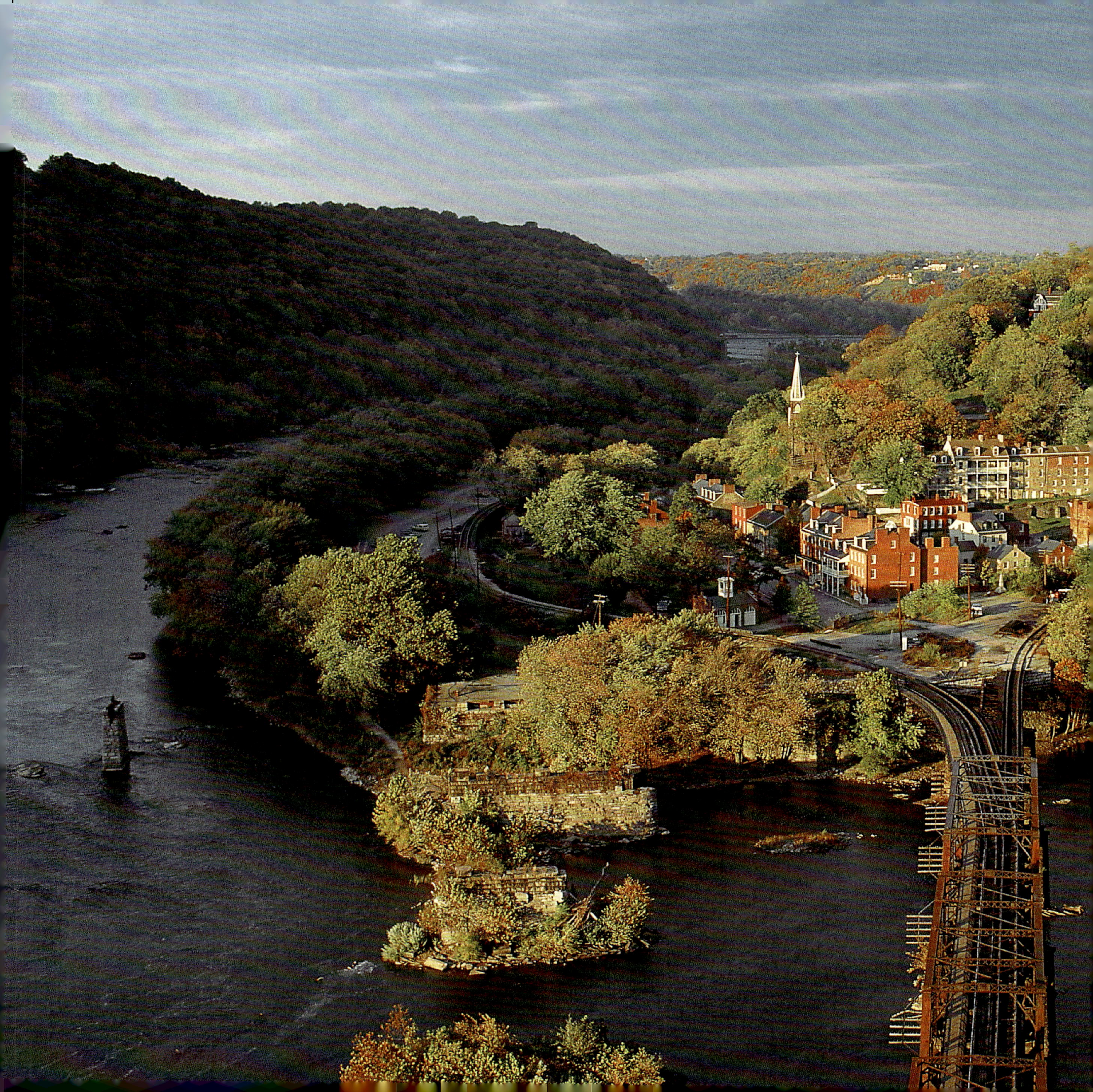

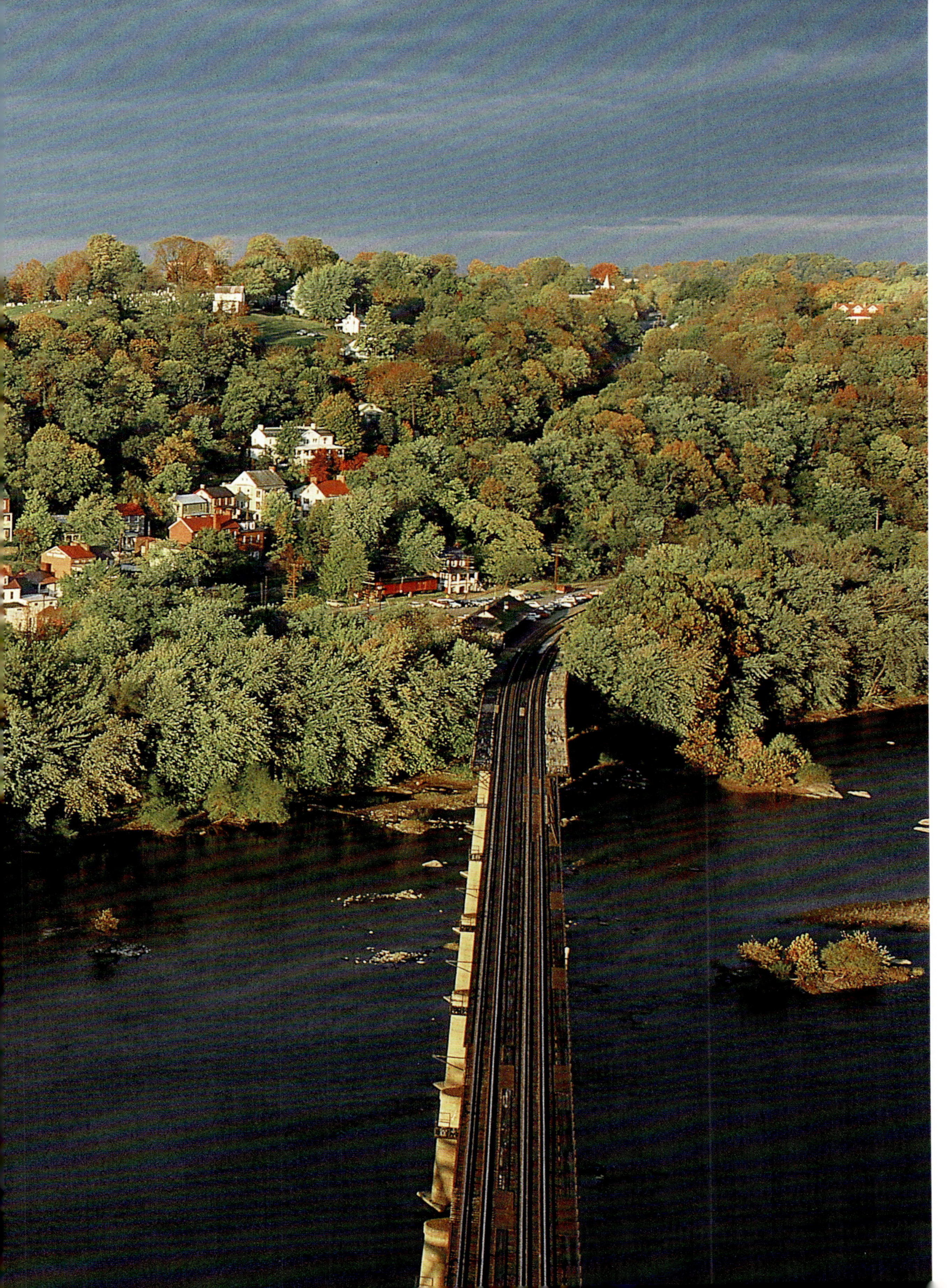

Harpers Ferry National Historic Park lies where Maryland meets Virginia and West Virginia, at the confluence of the Potomac and Shenandoah rivers. From here, John Brown plotted to free the slaves in 1859. Five years later, Union General Philip H. Sheridan used the town as a staging ground for his attack on Confederate troops. Both before and after, the town served as a hub for industry and transportation, including one of America's first railroads.

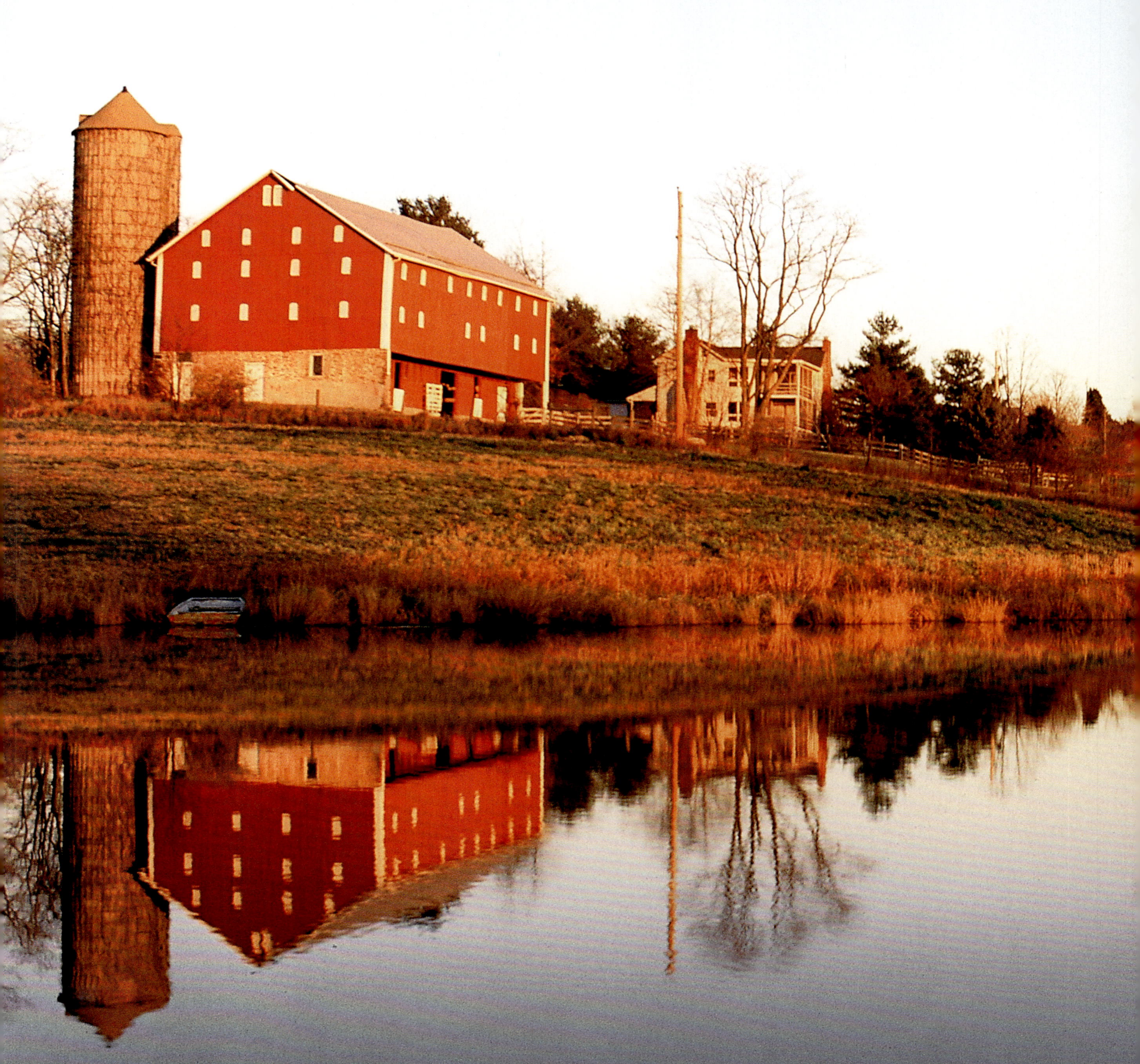

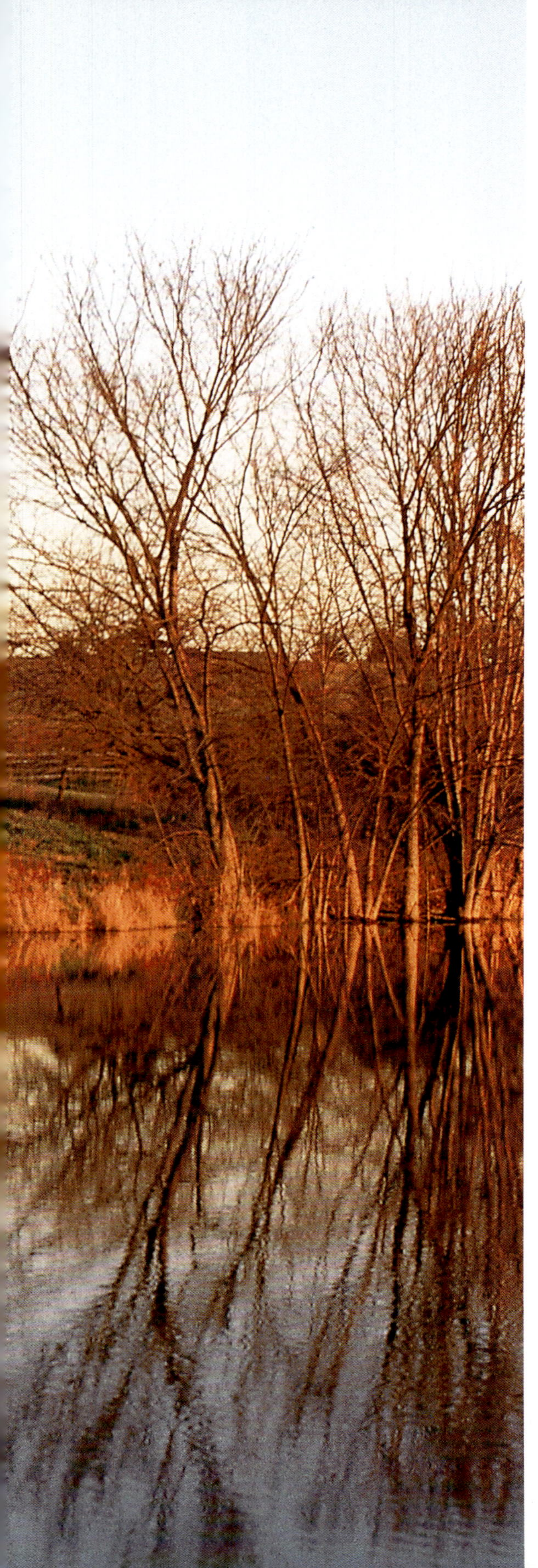

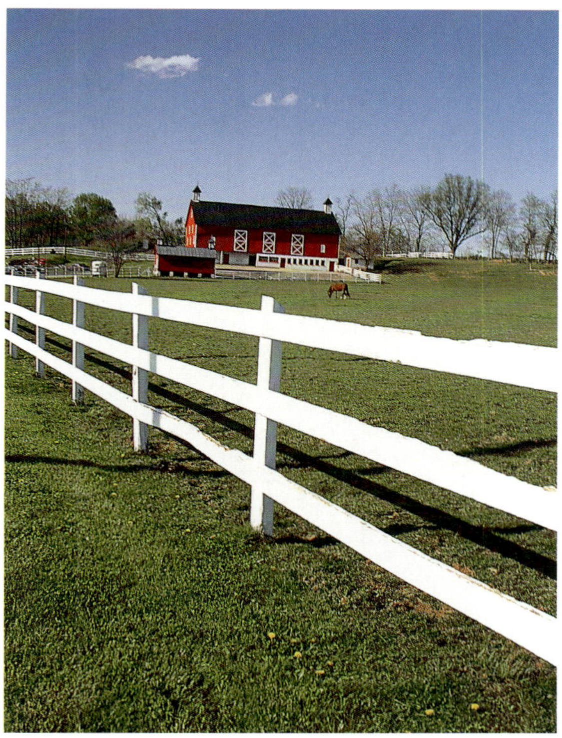

Maryland attracted growing numbers of settlers from the mid-1600s to the mid-1700s, most drawn by the promise of plentiful land. Named for Queen Henrietta Maria, wife of King Charles I, Maryland became the seventh state in the Union on April 28, 1788.

There are more than 12,000 farms in Maryland, comprising one-third of the state's total area. About 85 percent of these farms are owned by families or individuals, but that may change in the near future—the average age of a Maryland farmer is over 55.

OVERLEAF
Ships had already been docking here for more than a century when Baltimore was founded in 1729. With more than 40 million tons of cargo passing through each year, the city is now the fourth-busiest port in the nation.

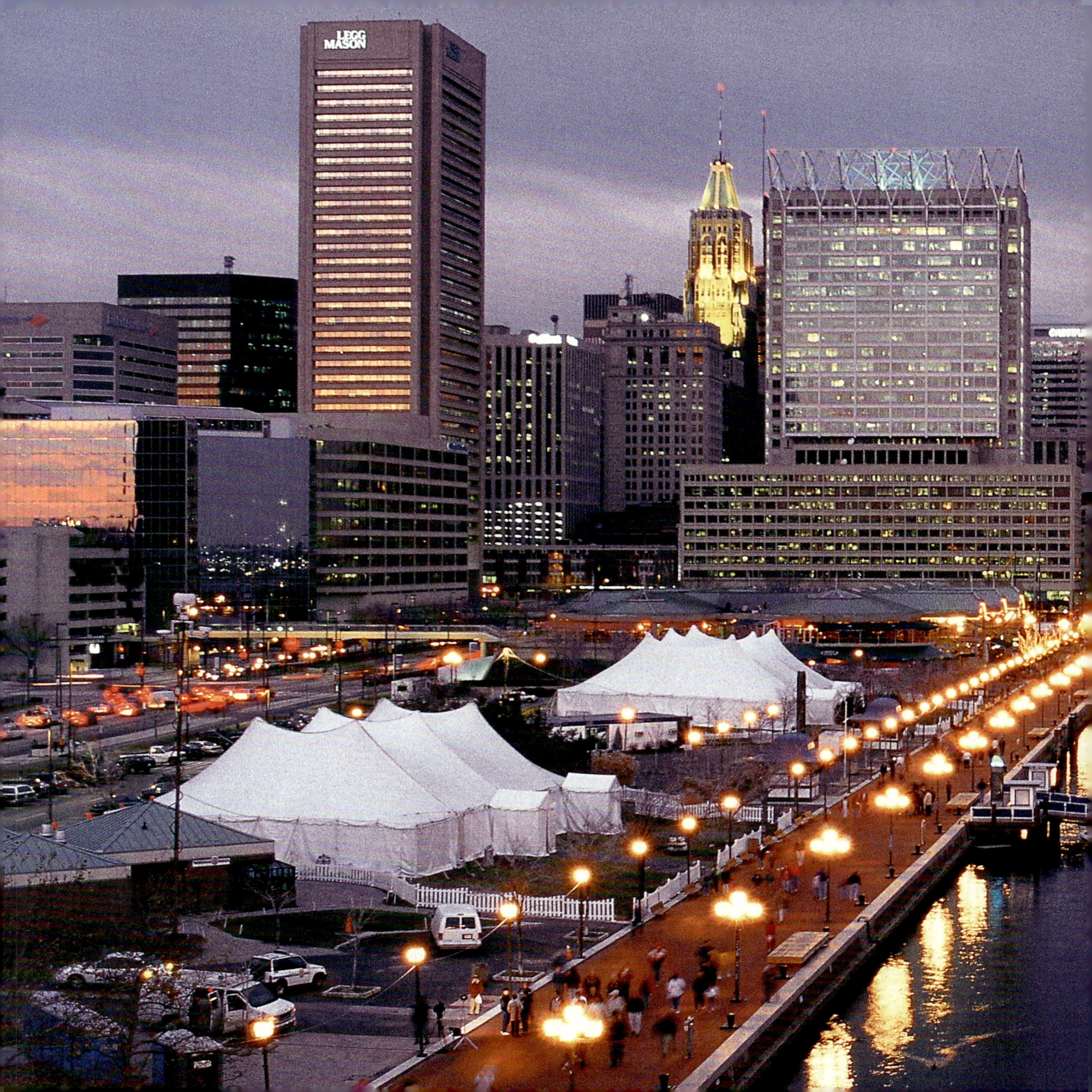
LEGG
MASON

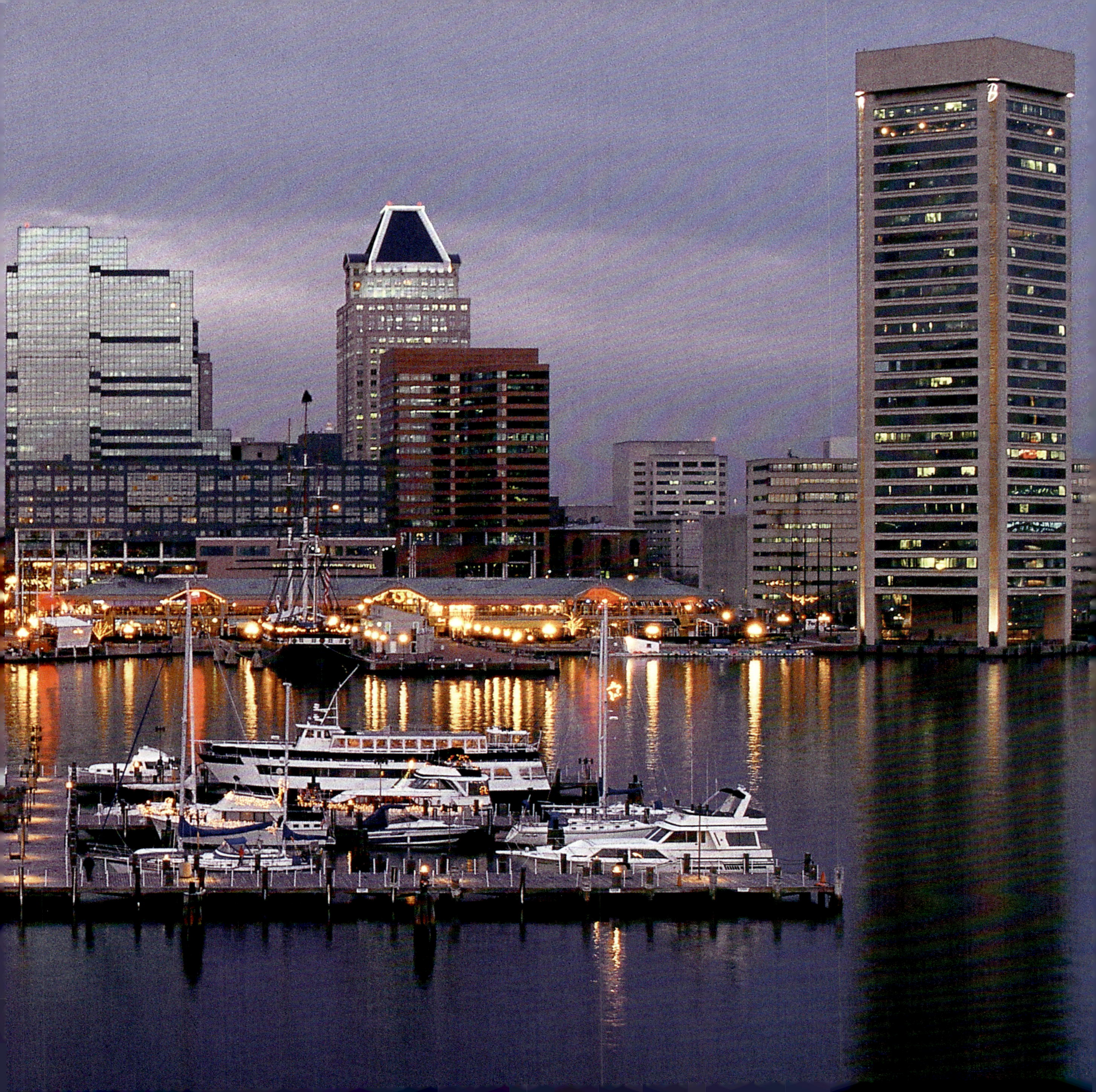

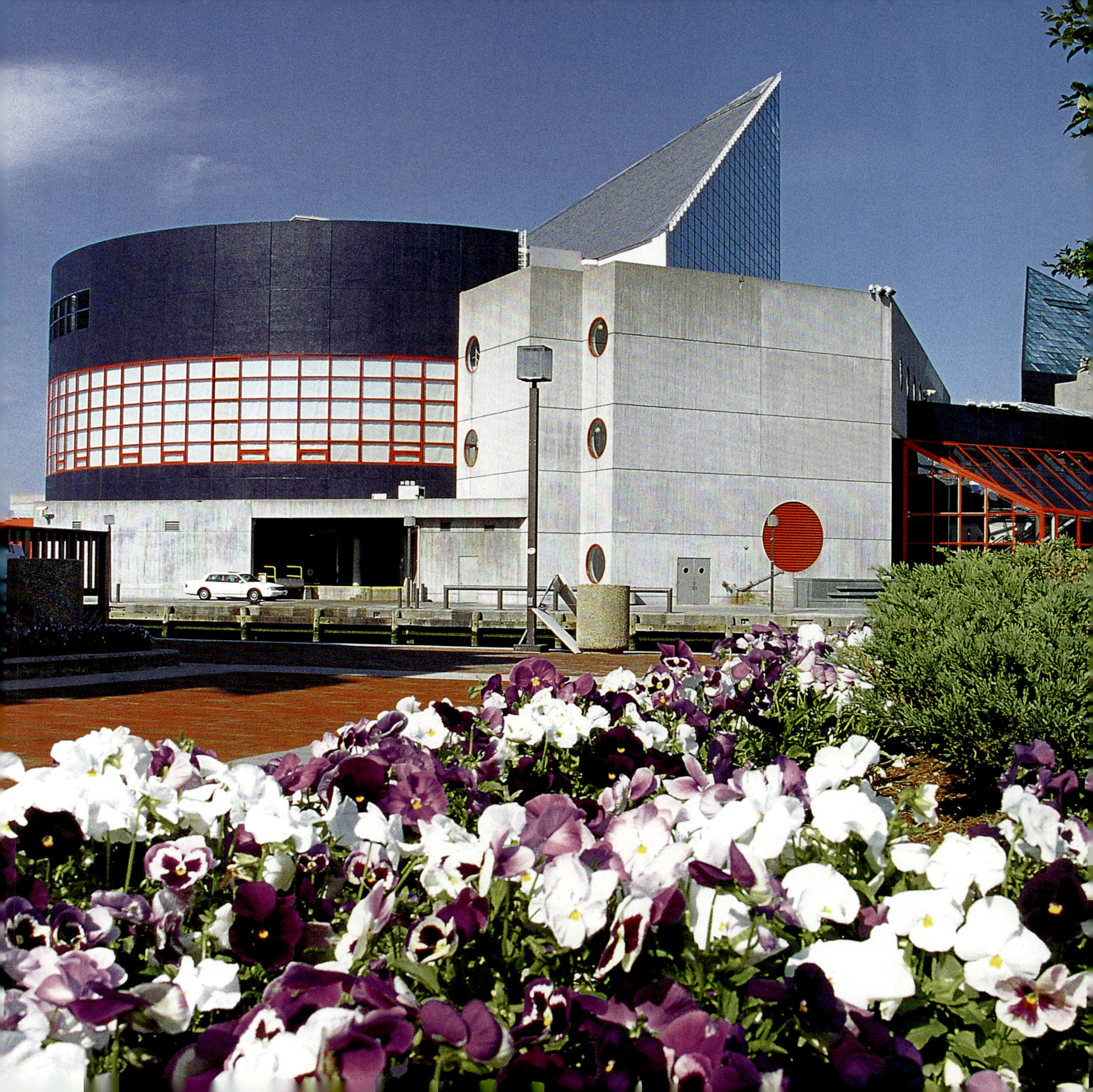

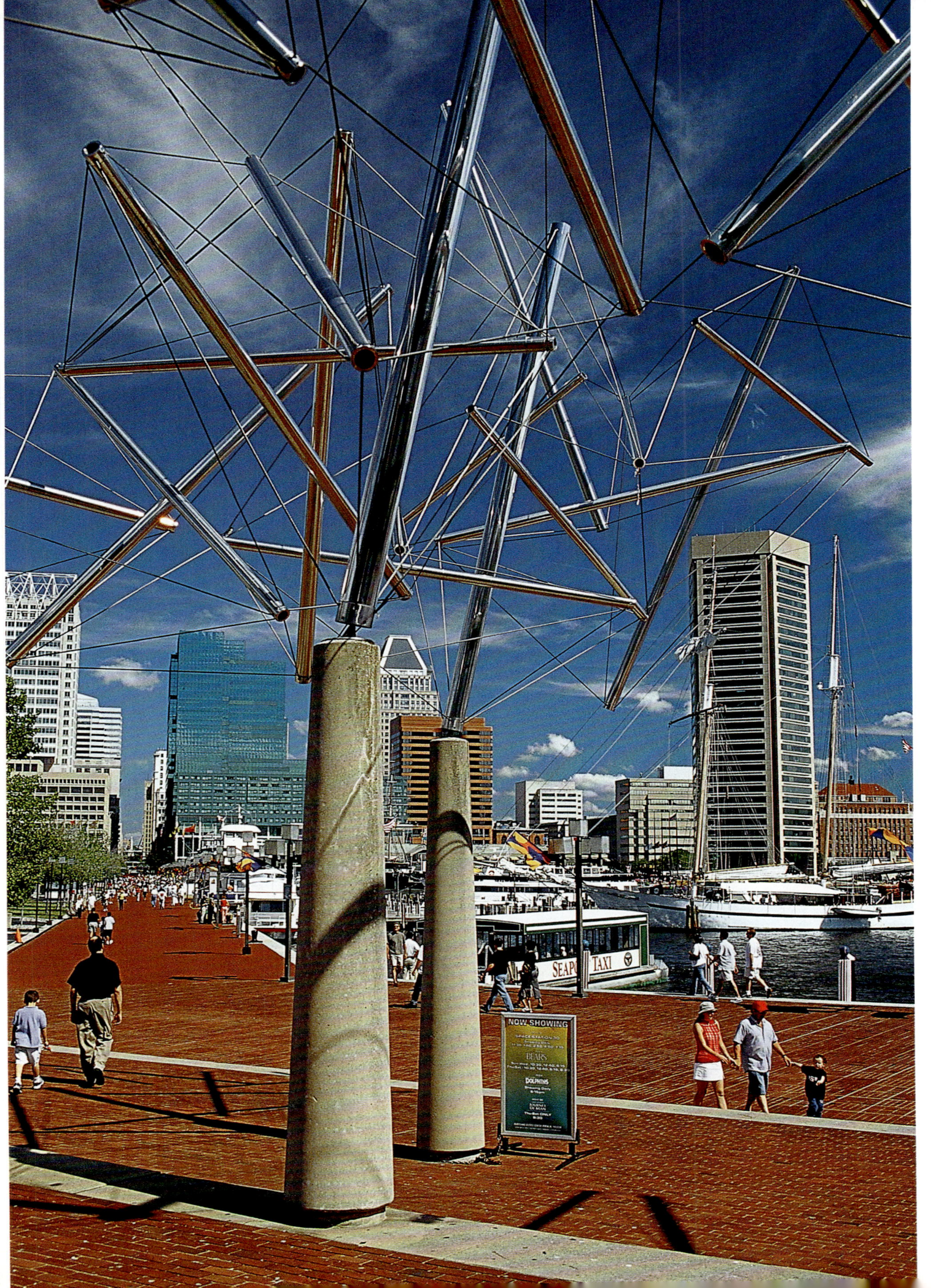

One of America's largest commercial centers in the nineteenth century, Baltimore was home to countless innovators and inventors. The first electric refrigerator was built here by Thomas Moore in 1803. The first American umbrella factory opened its doors in 1828 and the first candy factory produced licorice in 1869.

Facing Page
Explore the jungles of the Amazon, watch 600 creatures of the Atlantic coral reef, or follow the antics of seahorses and sea dragons. From the rainforest to the ocean depths, the National Aquarium in Baltimore has offered sightseers a closeup look at the ocean since 1981.

Many of Baltimore's attractions are clustered around the vibrant Inner Harbor, redeveloped in the 1970s. More than 13 million people each year now visit, drawn in part by the area's street entertainers, outdoor concerts, festivals, and parades. Visitors can rent paddle boats, charter fishing tours, or don skates at the outdoor skating rink.

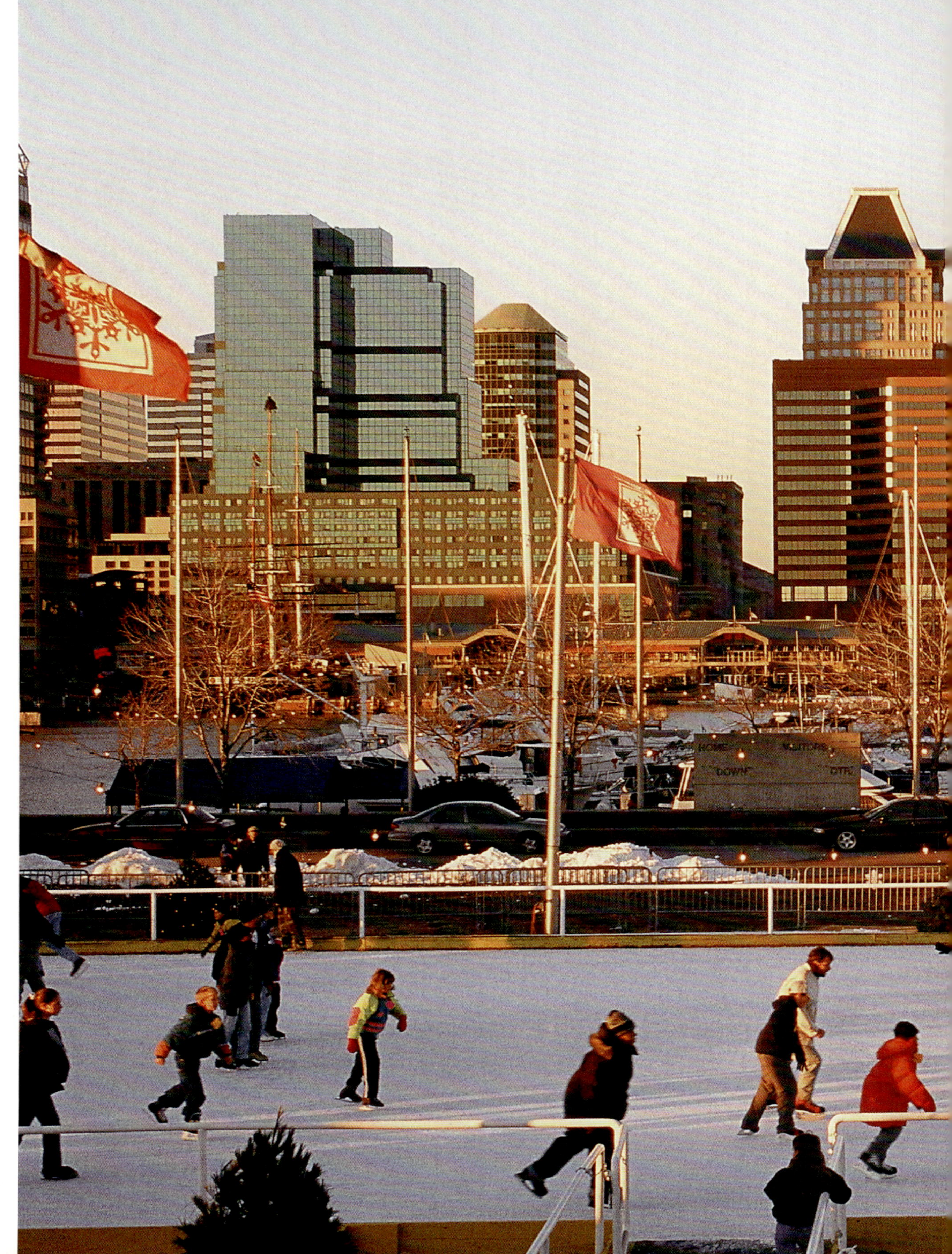

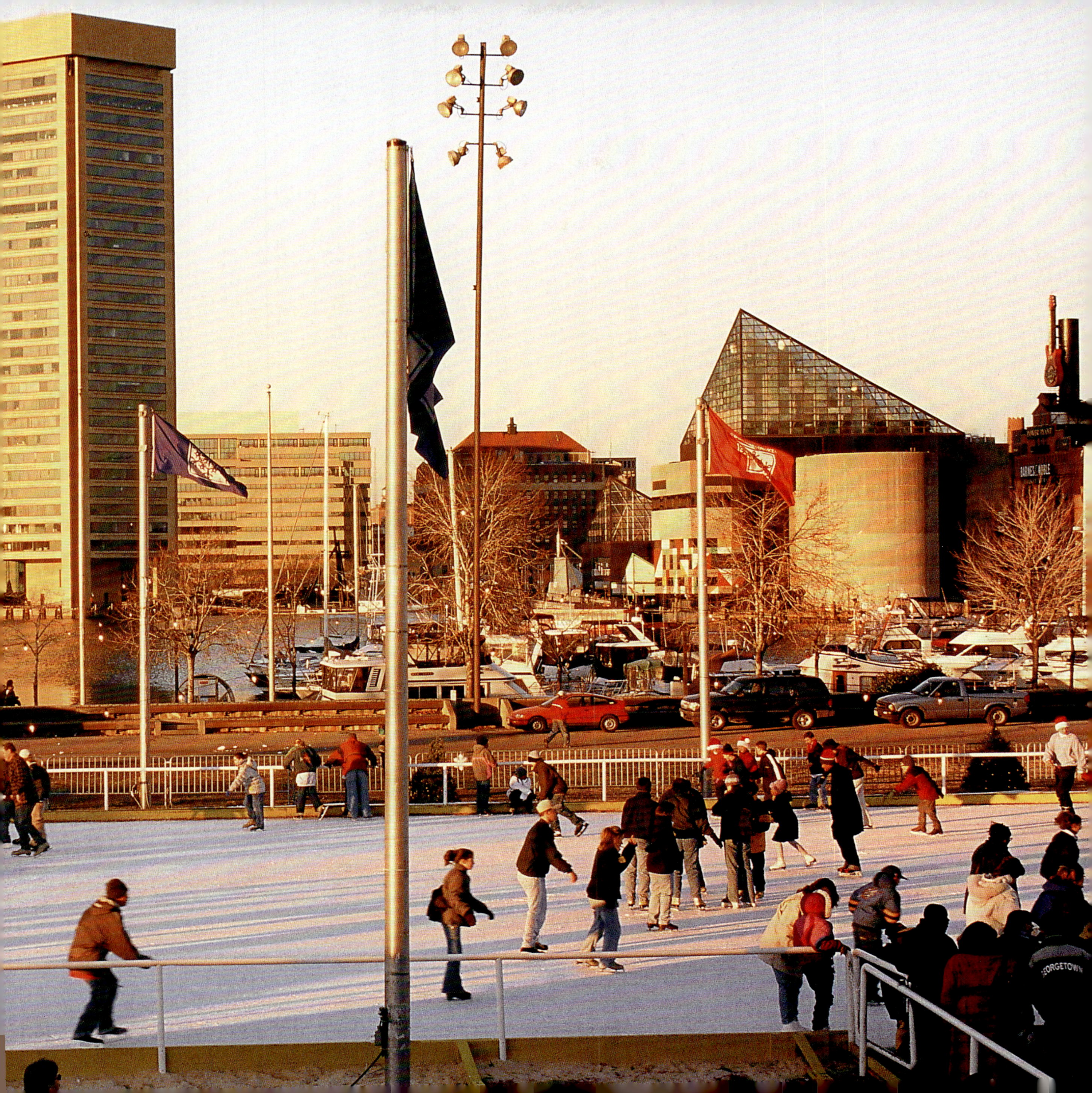

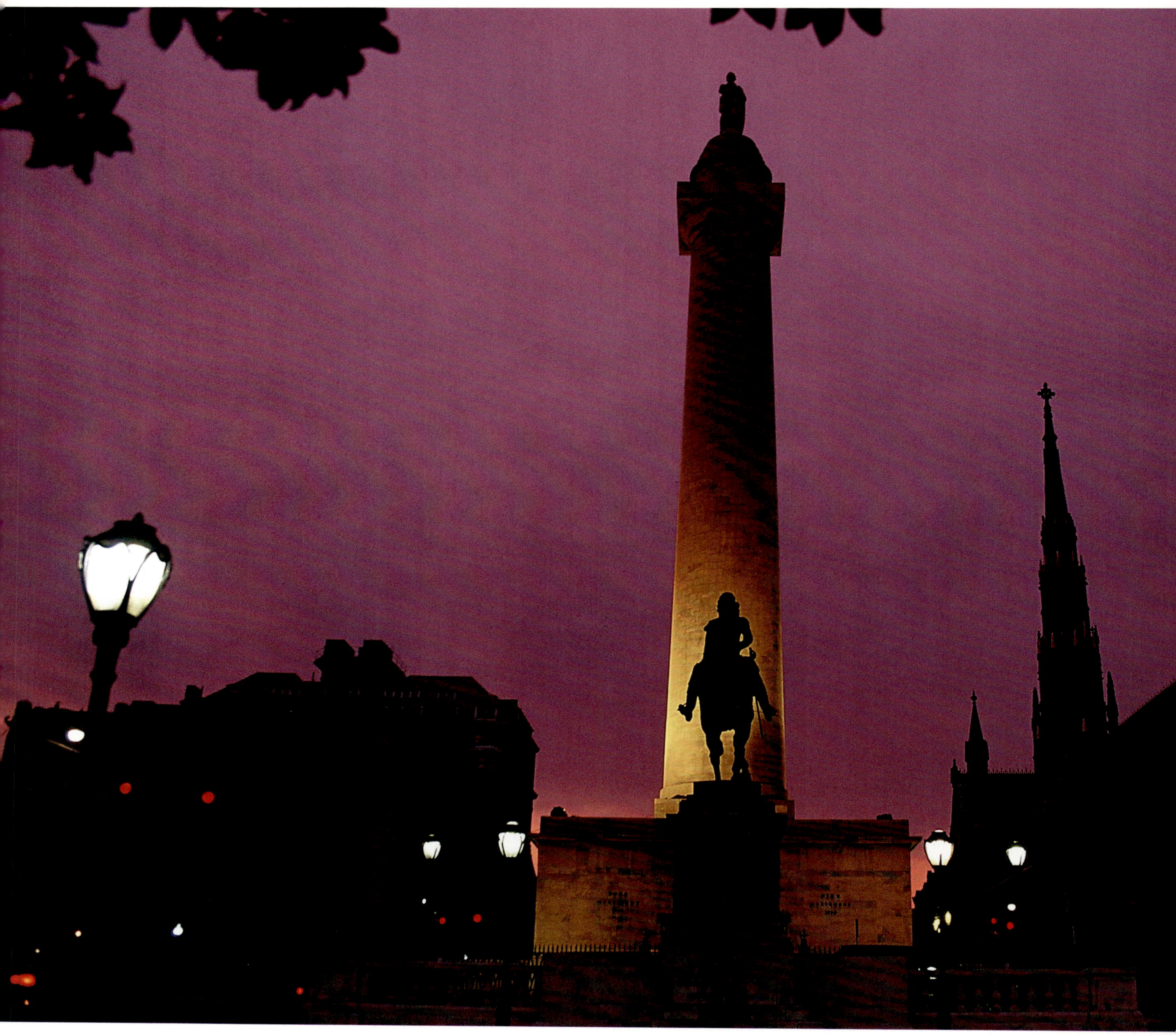

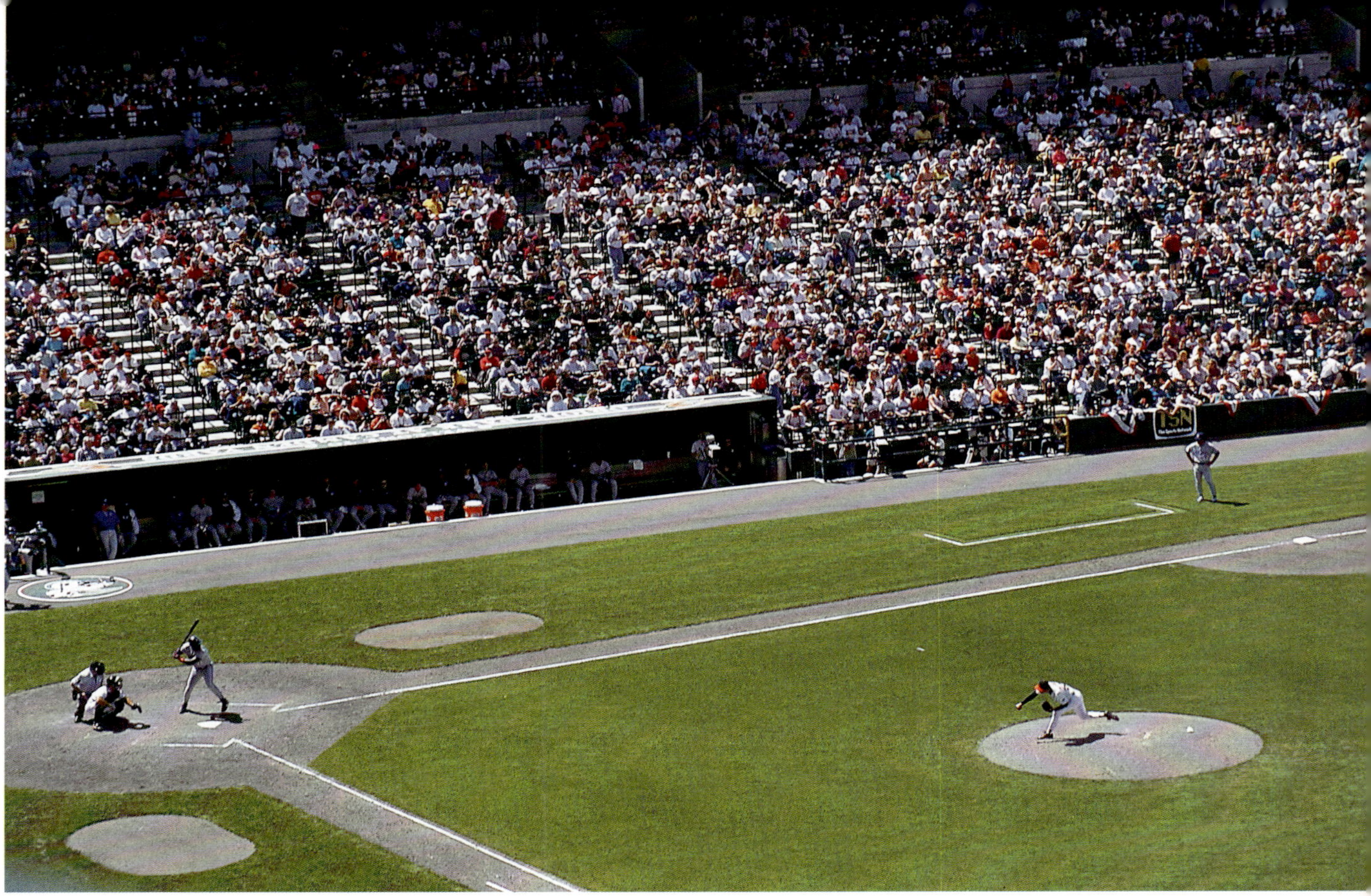

Oriole Park, home of the Baltimore Orioles baseball team, is only a short walk from the city's Inner Harbor. It was built in 1992 on the site of a former railway yard and seats more than 48,000 fans. Coincidentally, the ballpark is only two blocks from the birthplace of baseball legend Babe Ruth.

Only ten years after the president's death, Baltimore citizens began planning a monument to George Washington. They raised $100,000 and by 1815, architect Robert Mills was overseeing the construction of a 160-foot column, eventually to be crowned with a 16-foot marble sculpture by Italy's Enrico Causici.

Johns Hopkins University in Baltimore opened in 1876 with a unique mission. The school aimed to not only enhance students' knowledge, but to increase the knowledge of humankind through research. The university bears the name of railway baron Johns Hopkins, who left a bequest of $7 million to fund a school and a hospital. At the time, it was the largest bequest in American history.

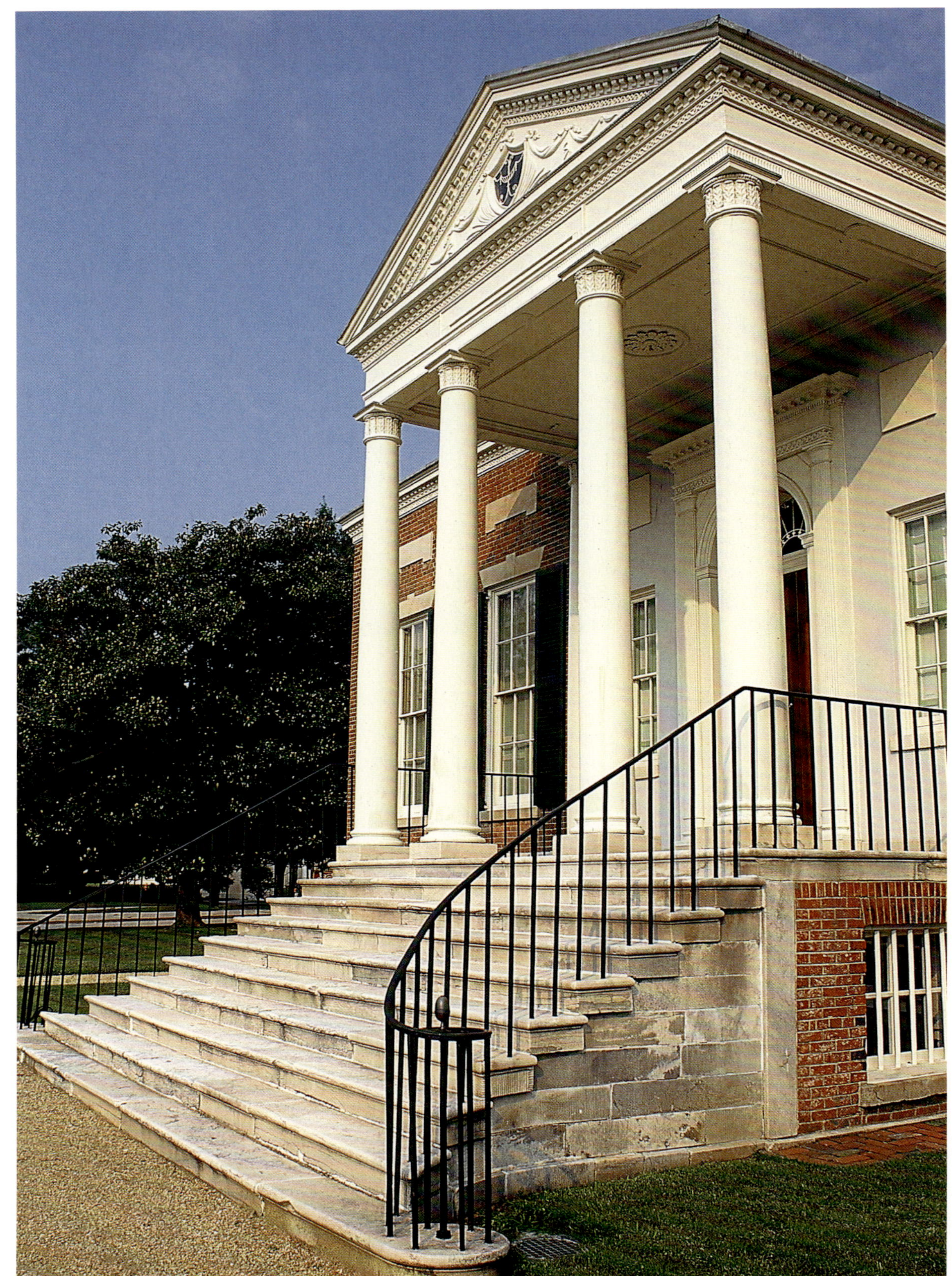

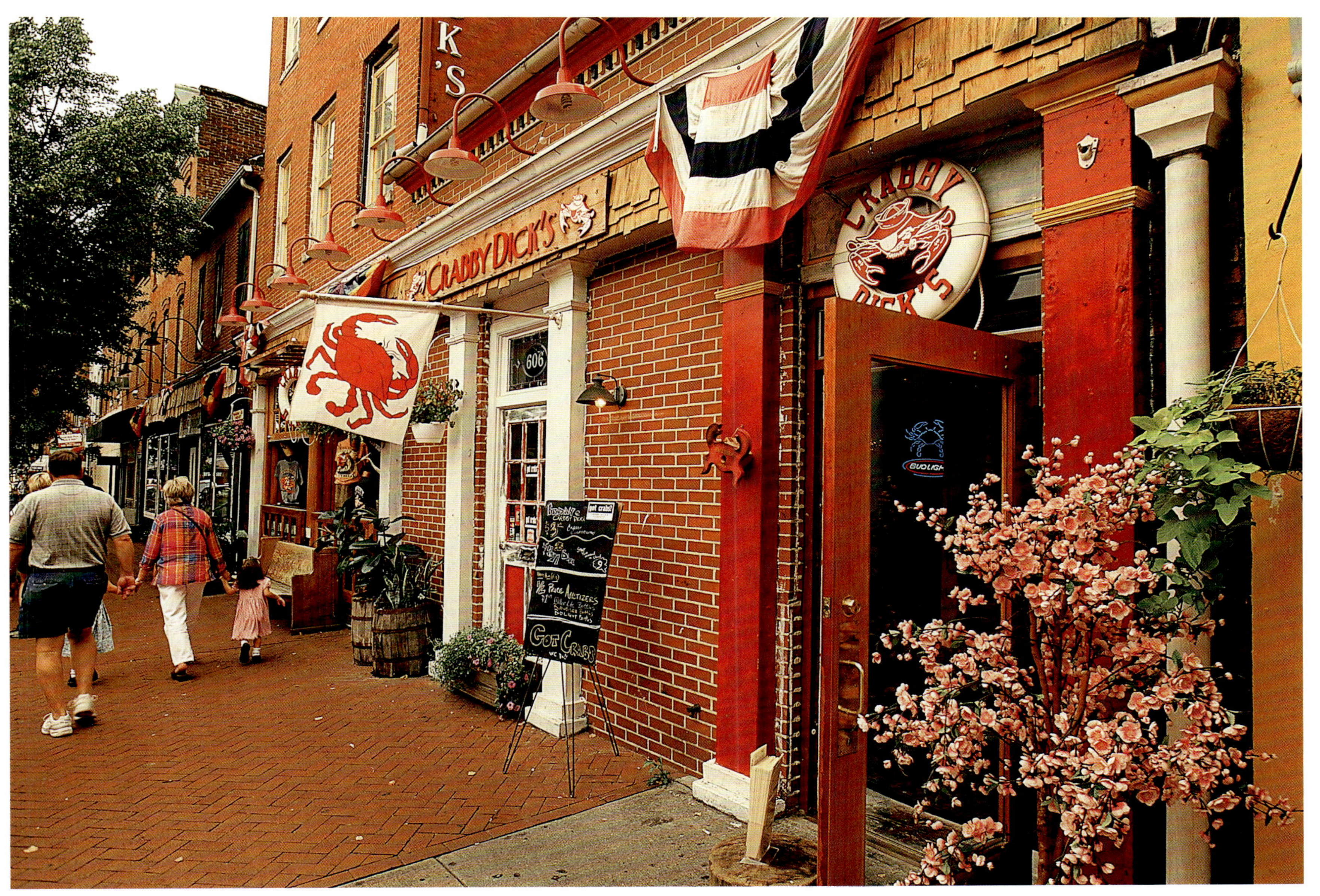

History is not the only attraction in Fells Point. Cafés, bistros, and nightspots now occupy historic commercial spaces, making this a favorite evening destination for both visitors and city dwellers. Annual celebrations, such as the Fells Point Fun Festival and the Olde Fashioned Candlelight Christmas festivities, also draw thousands of revelers.

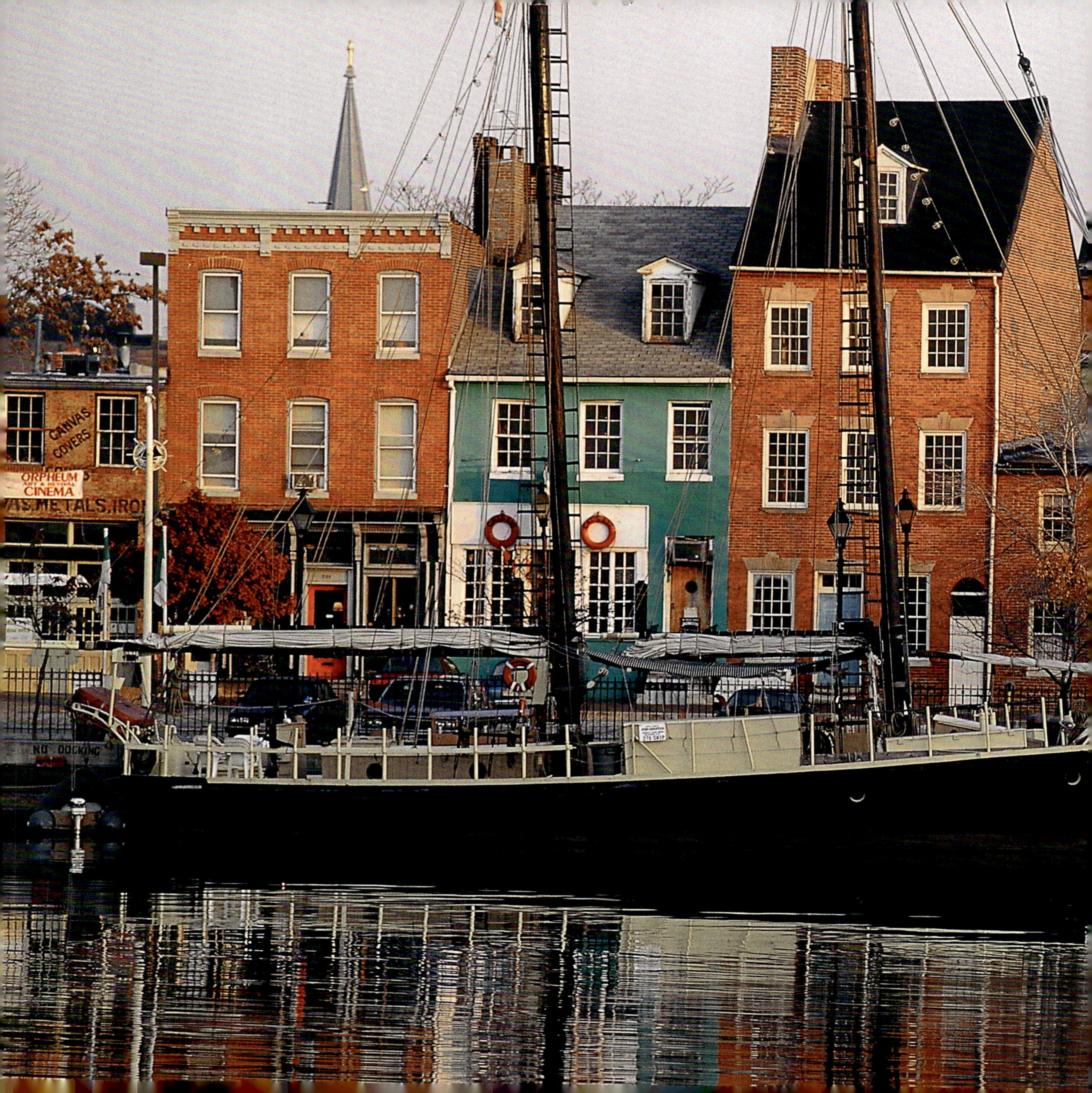
CANVAS
COVERS
ORPHEUM
CINEMA
NO DOCKING

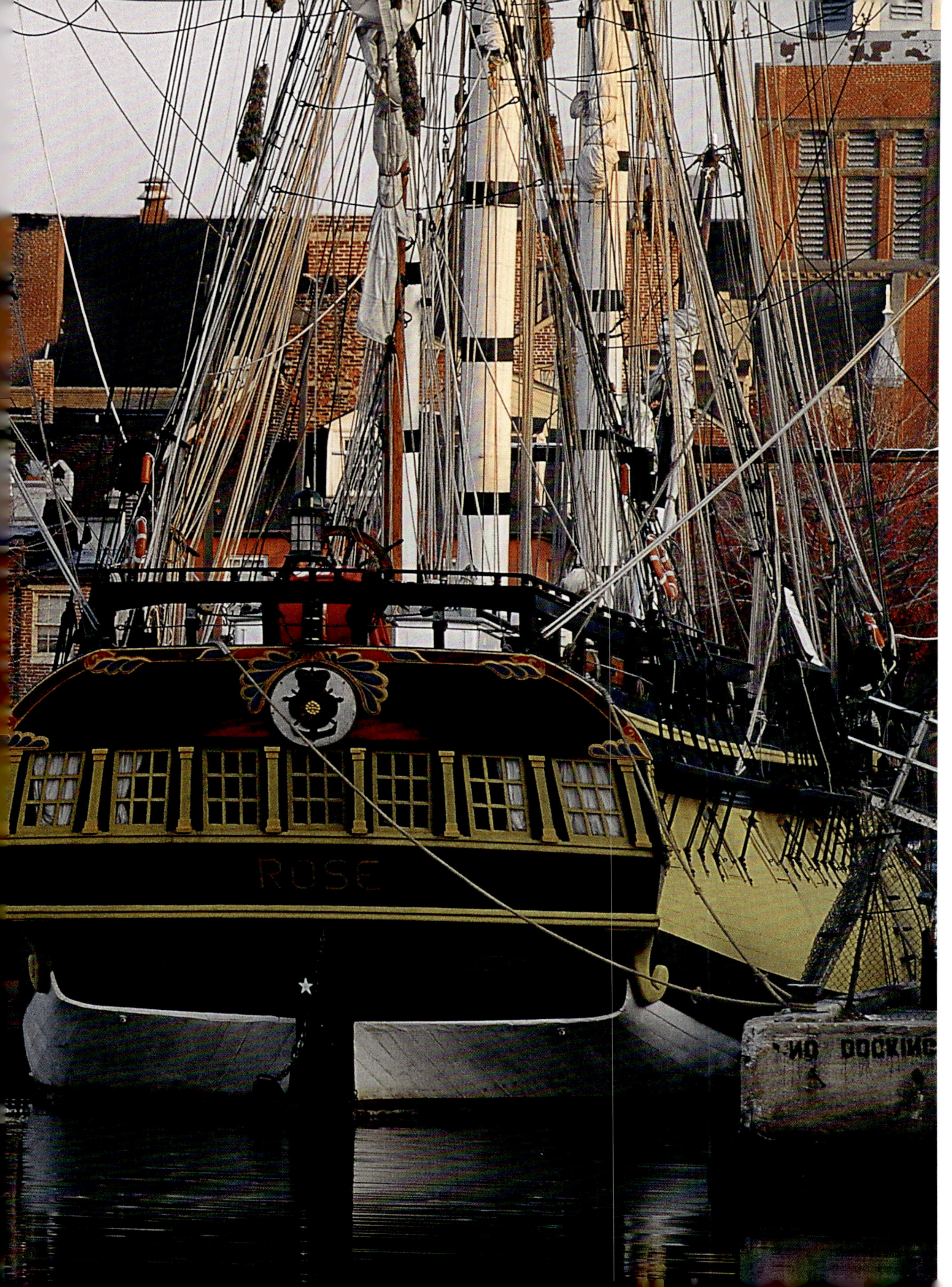

Listed on the National Register of Historic Places, Fells Point is the oldest neighborhood in Baltimore. Seeing opportunities for shipbuilding in the region, English settler William Fell bought land here in 1726. His wife and son sold parcels to entrepreneurs and land speculators after William's death in the mid-1700s. The oldest building still standing dates from 1765.

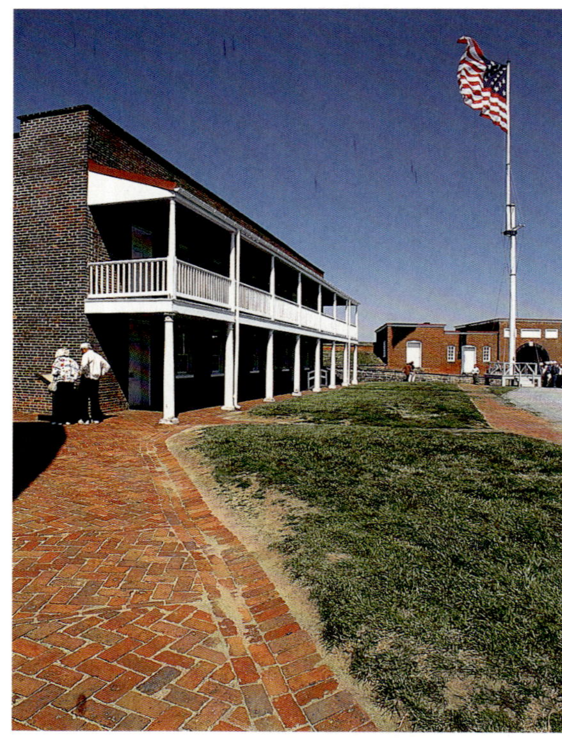

In 1814, Francis Scott Key saw the forces of Fort McHenry valiantly guard Baltimore's harbor against the British, which inspired him to write "The Star-Spangled Banner." At Fort McHenry National Monument and Historic Shrine, visitors can examine reminders of the War of 1812—early flags, soldiers' uniforms, and cannons.

From cacti and palm trees to rainforest ferns and tropical blooms, the Baltimore Conservatory and Botanic Gardens feature plants from the city's backyard and from around the world. Baltimore's largest Easter egg hunt draws visitors each spring, and the holiday poinsettia display is the highlight of the winter season.

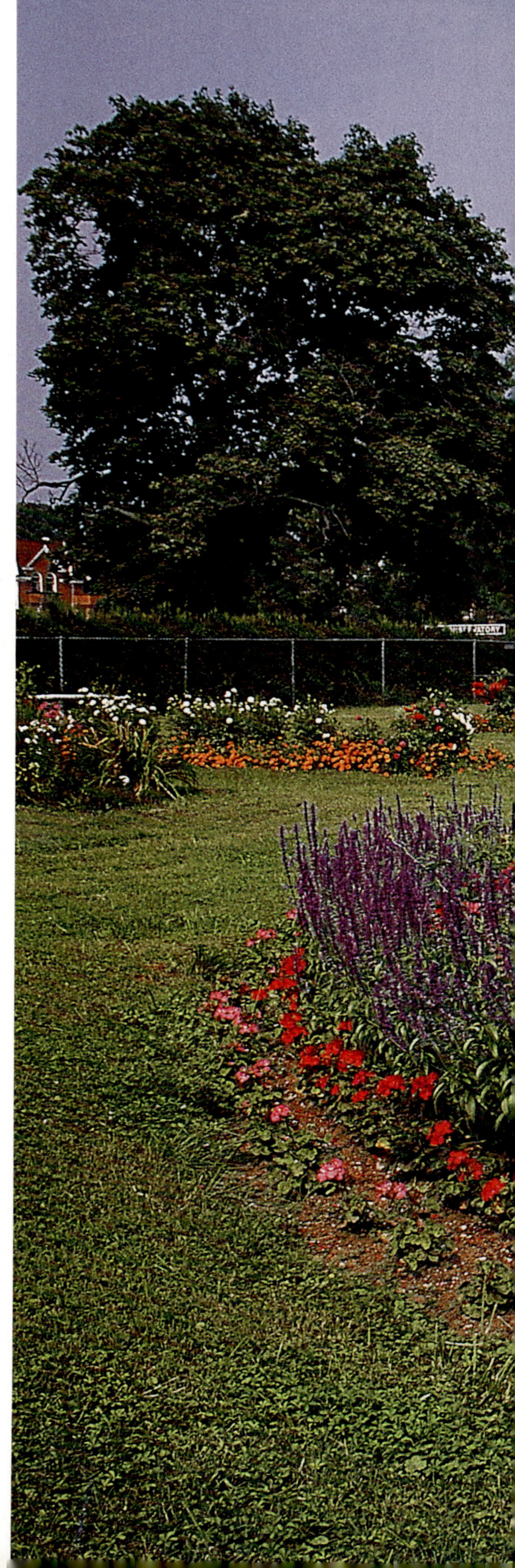

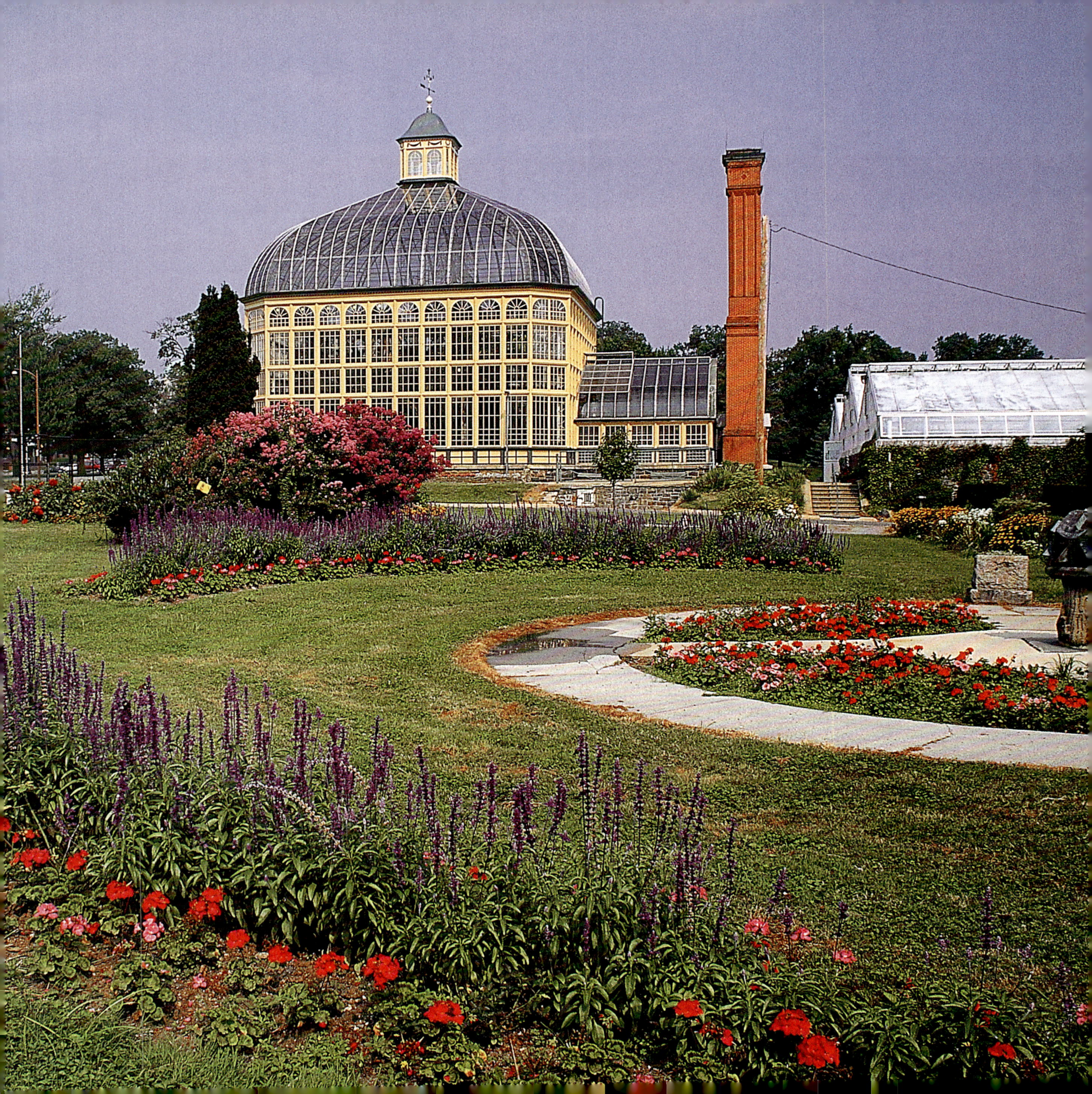

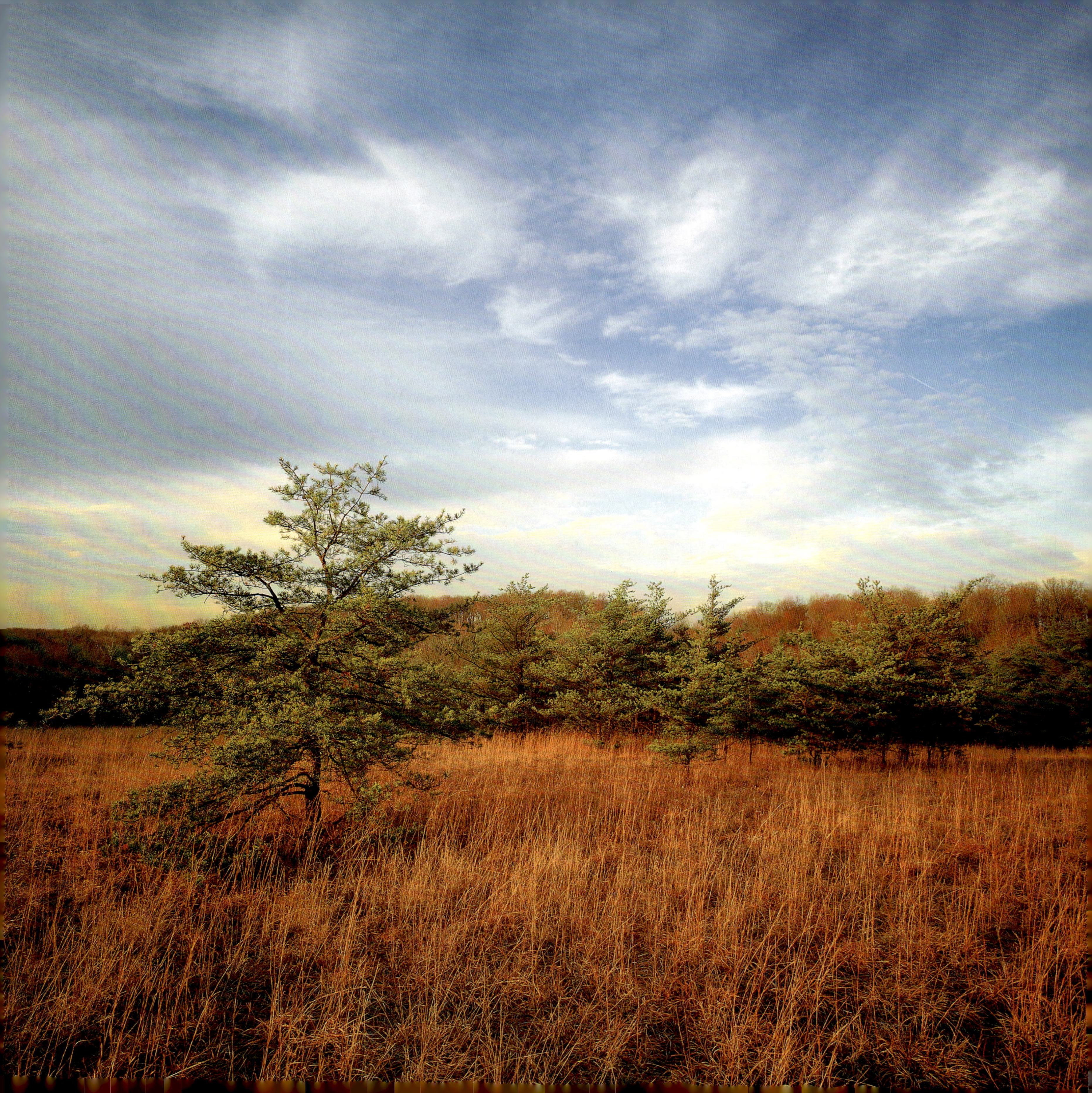

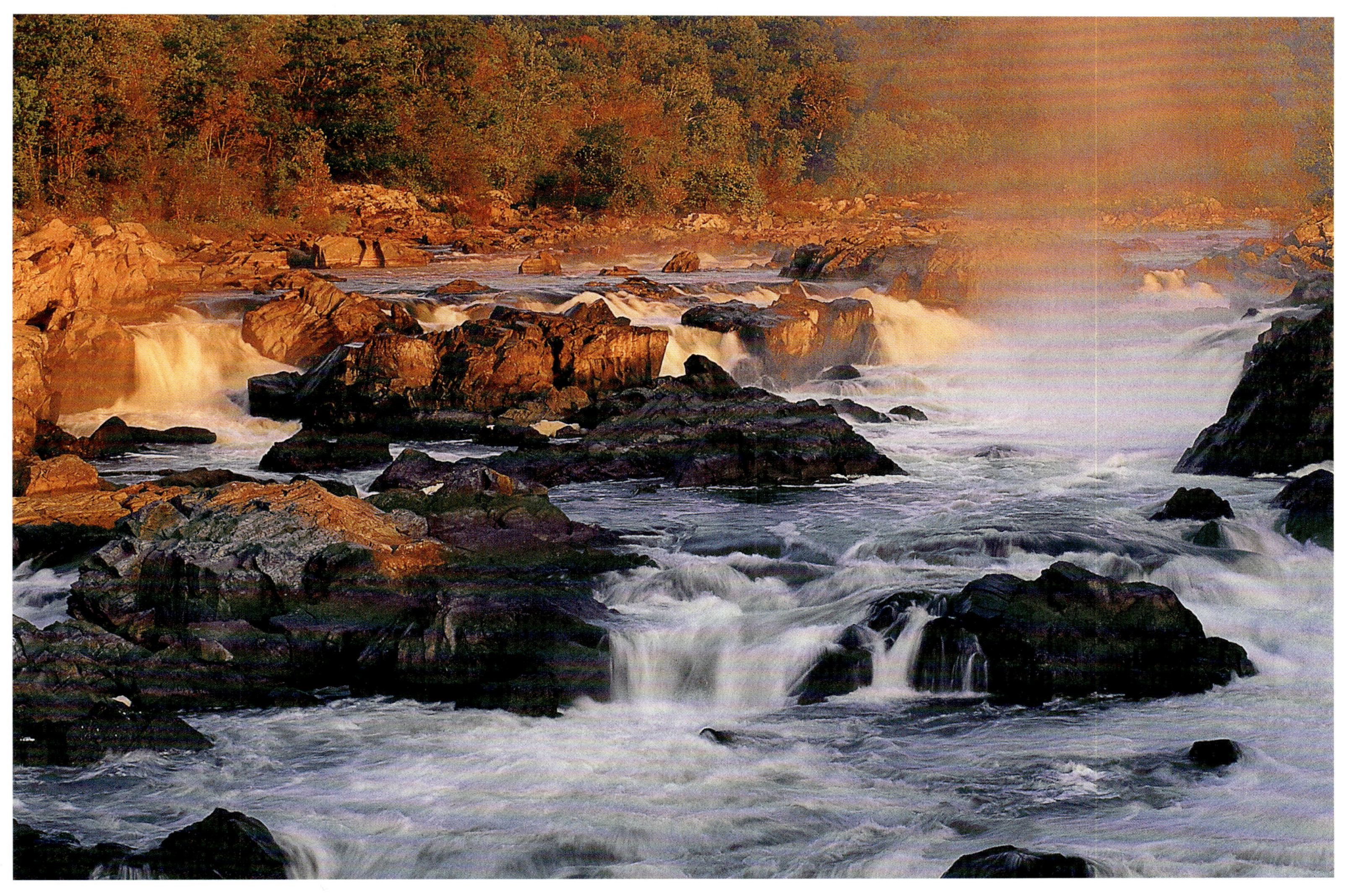

At Great Falls, the Potomac River churns through a narrow gorge, pouring over a series of 20 waterfalls within 3,500 feet. Paddlers brave some of these rapids in an annual race, challenging parts of the river with names such as Pummel Falls, the Double Pencil Sharpener, and the Horseshoe.

Soldiers Delight Natural Environmental Area protects a 1,900-acre serpentine barren. Formed mainly of easily eroded serpentinite, the sandy, infertile soil supports sparse vegetation, including 39 rare plant species. Seven miles of hiking trails allow visitors to experience the fragile ecosystem.

The overhangs and cracks of Carderock attract hundreds of rock climbers each summer to this part of the Chesapeake and Ohio Canal National Historic Park. About 35 routes provide challenges for both novice and expert climbers.

FACING PAGE
Opened in 1828, the Chesapeake and Ohio Canal follows the course of the Potomac River for more than 180 miles between Washington, D.C., and Cumberland, Maryland. Though the historic locks no longer serve the ships and coal barges, a national historic park offers a linear preserve for history buffs, hikers, cyclists, and paddlers.

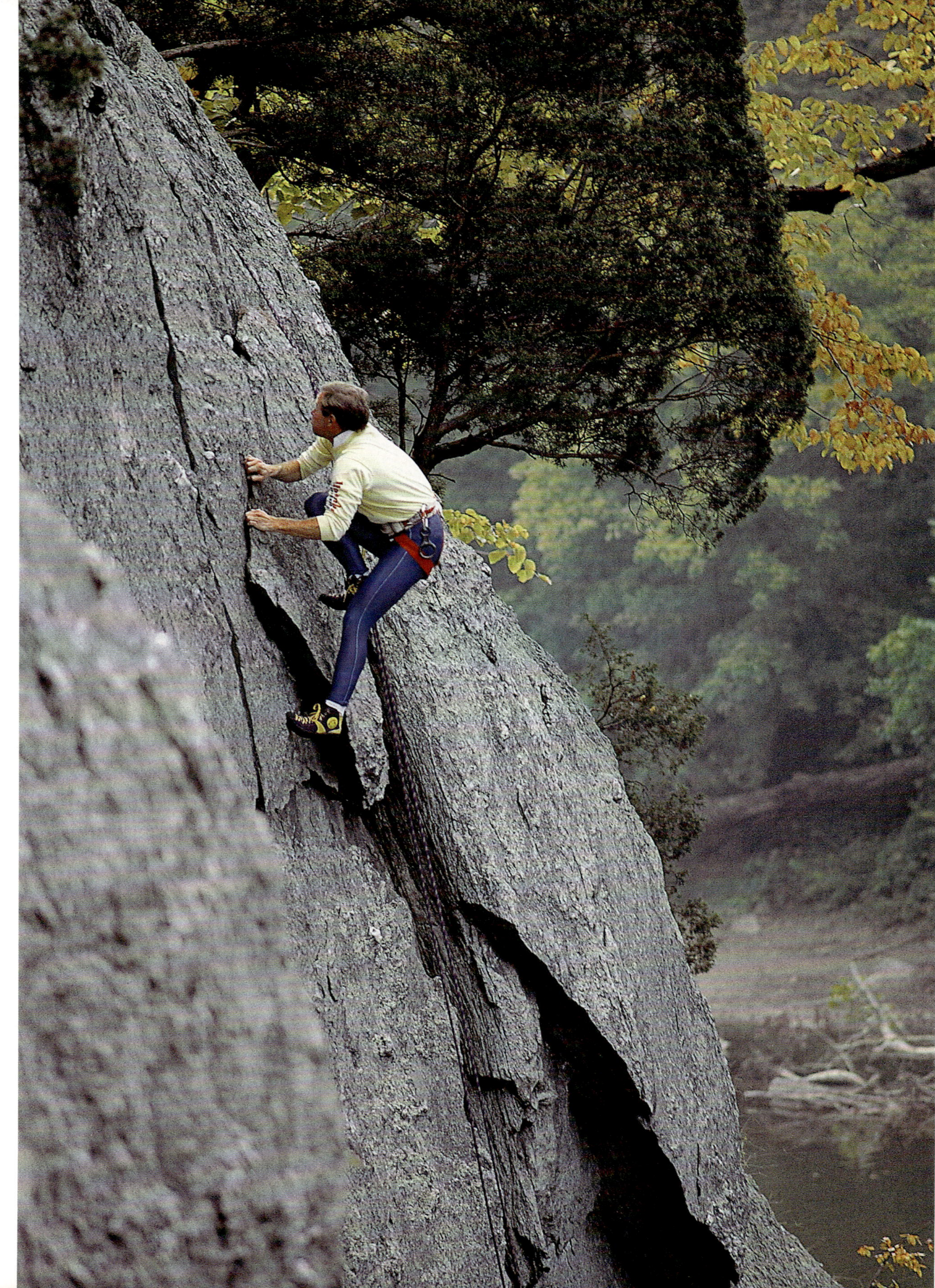

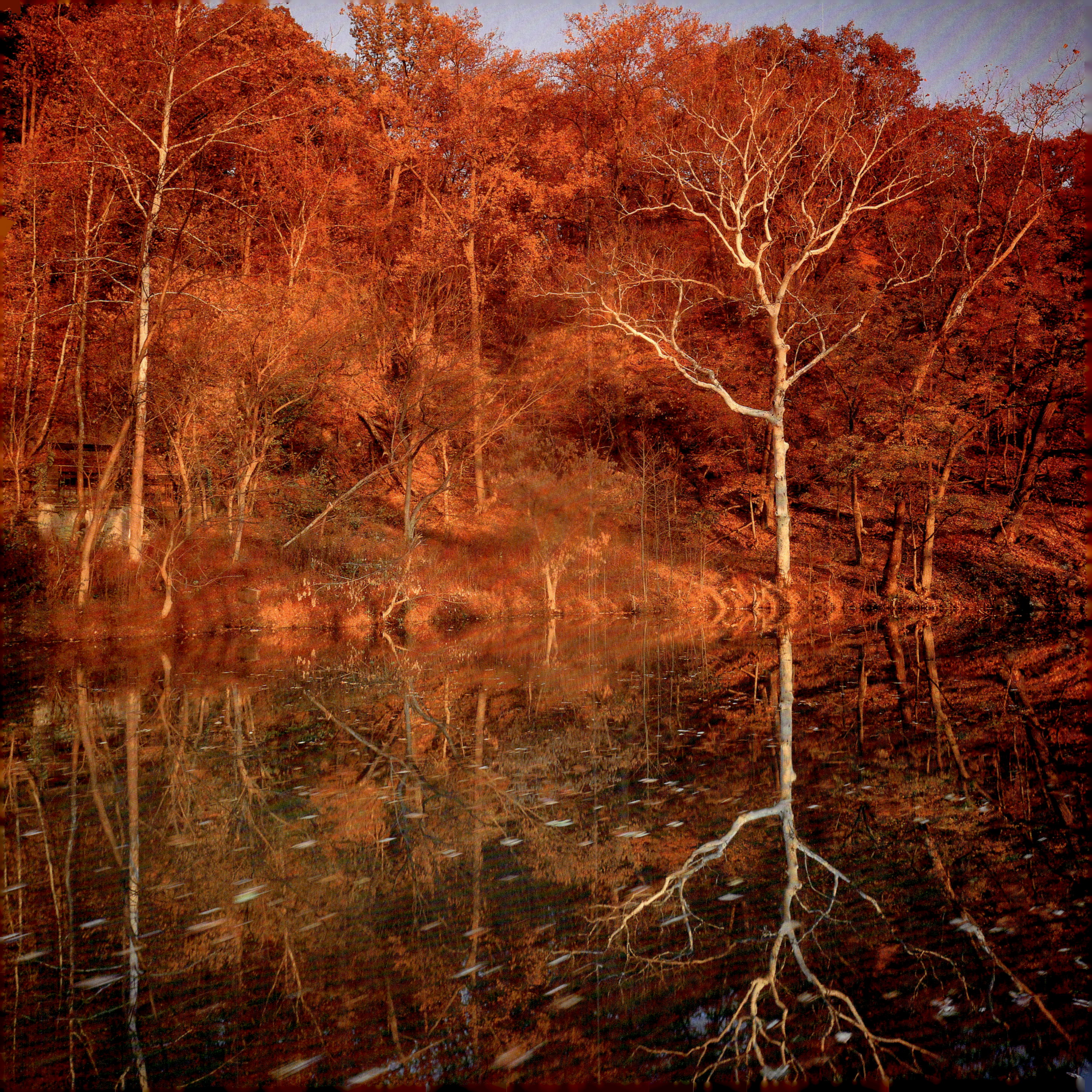

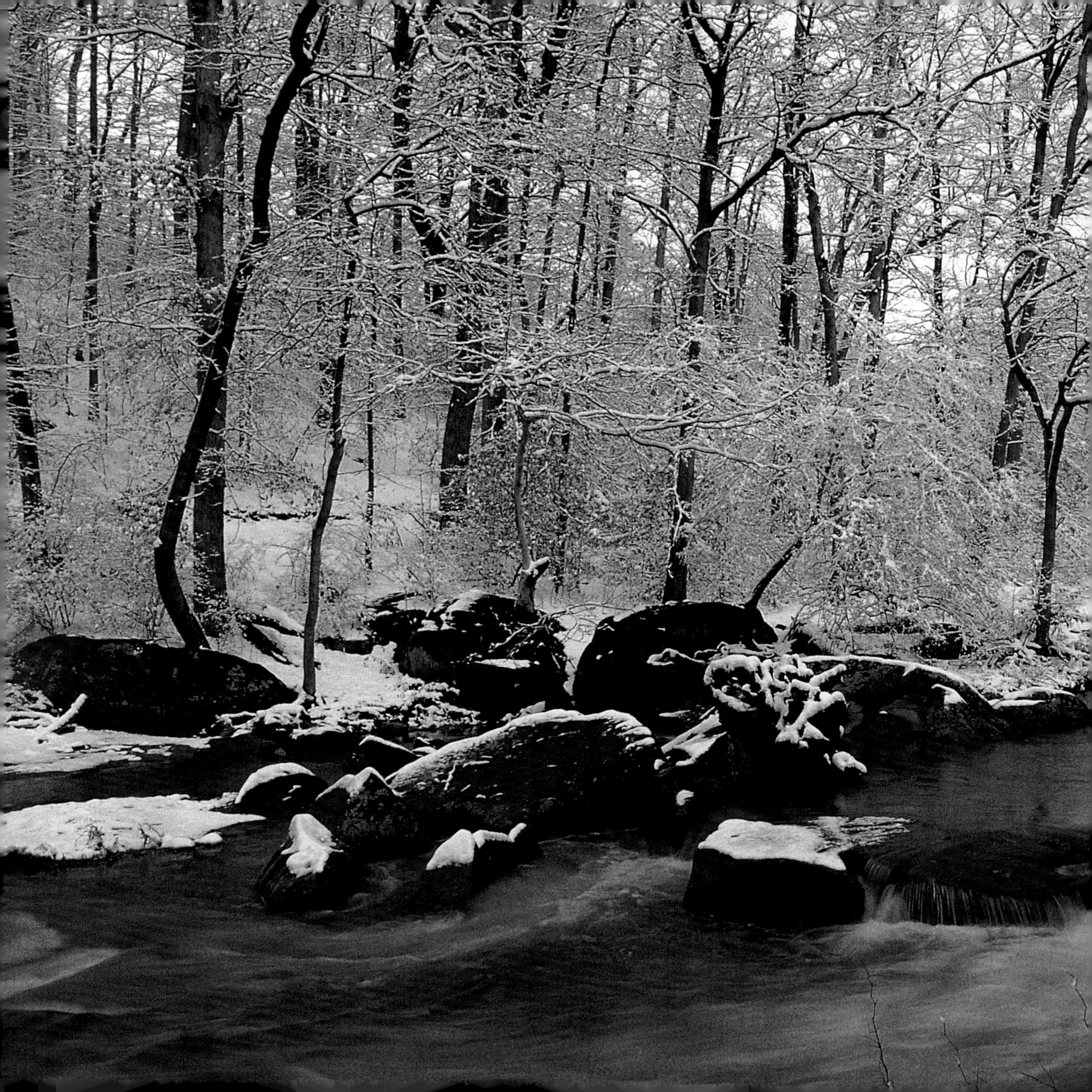

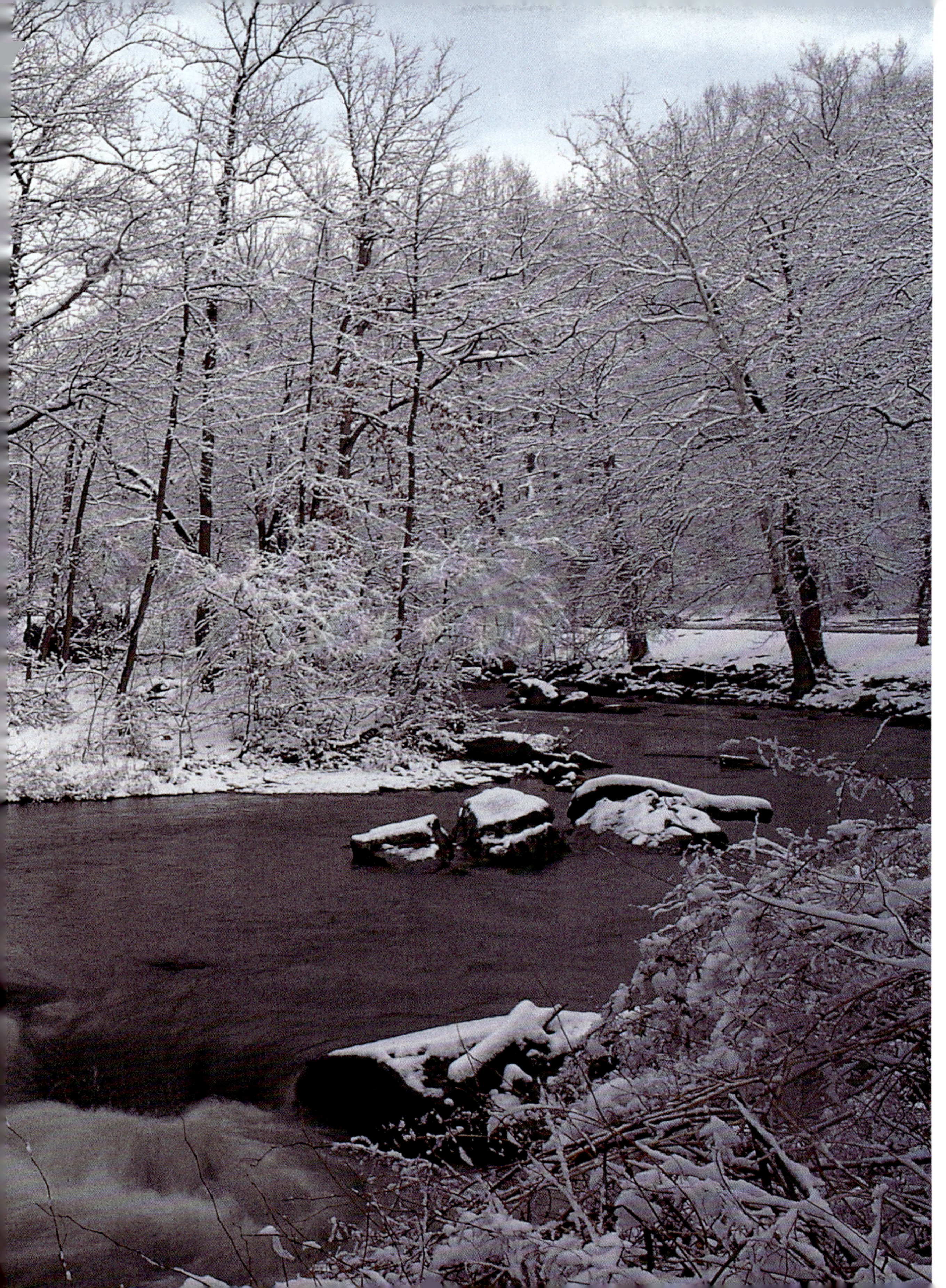

Rock Creek Park, a regional park in Maryland, connects to the larger National Park Service preserve in Washington, D.C. Woodlands and natural meadows provide refuge for a wide range of small mammal and bird species, while hiking trails, bridle paths, cycling routes, and picnic facilities cater to nearby city dwellers.

On the outskirts of Washington, D.C., Bethesda is home to the National Institute of Health, the National Library of Medicine, and the National Naval Medical Center. In fact, the city is named after a biblical place of healing. Bethesda is home to 97,000 residents and more than 300 restaurants and shops.

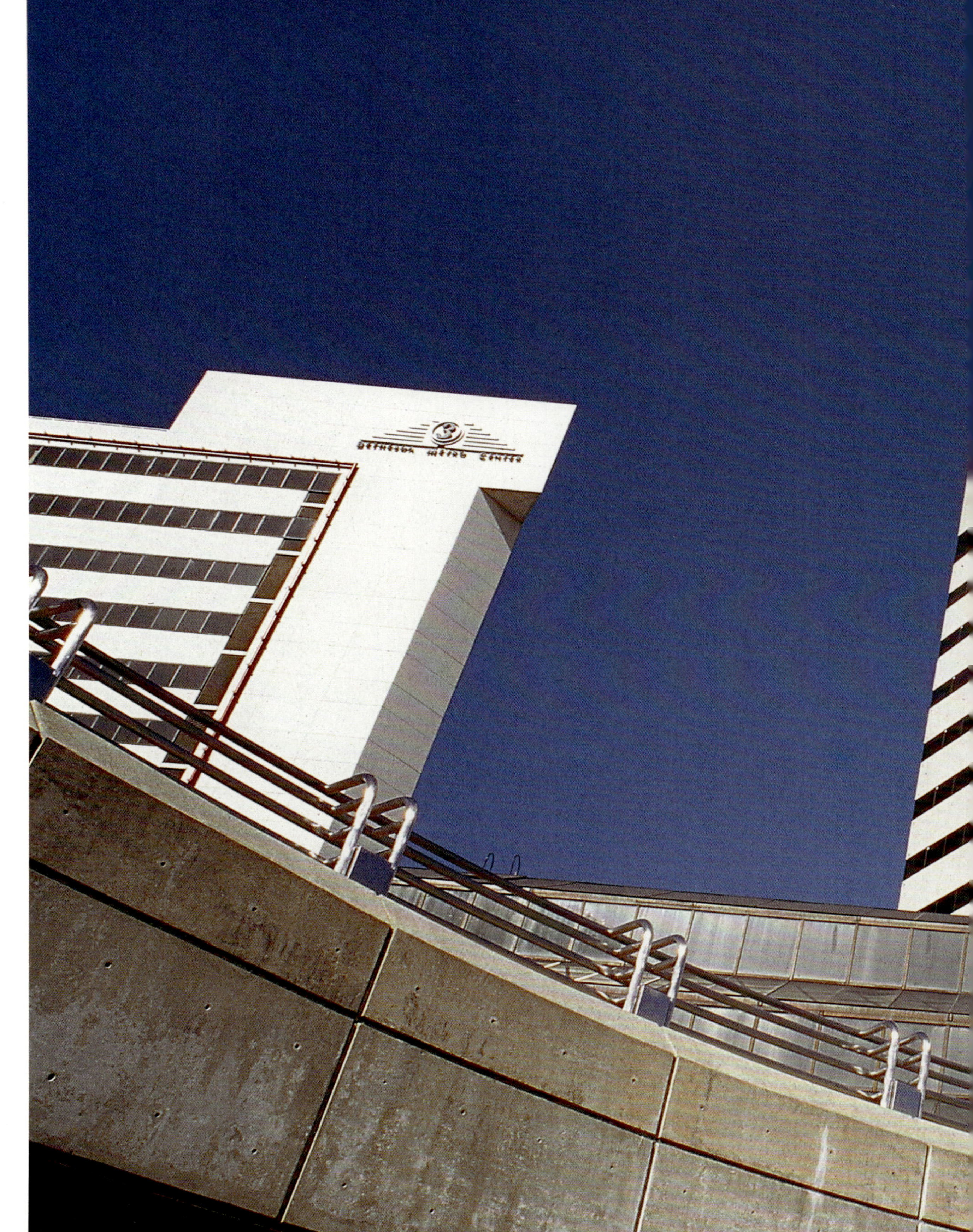

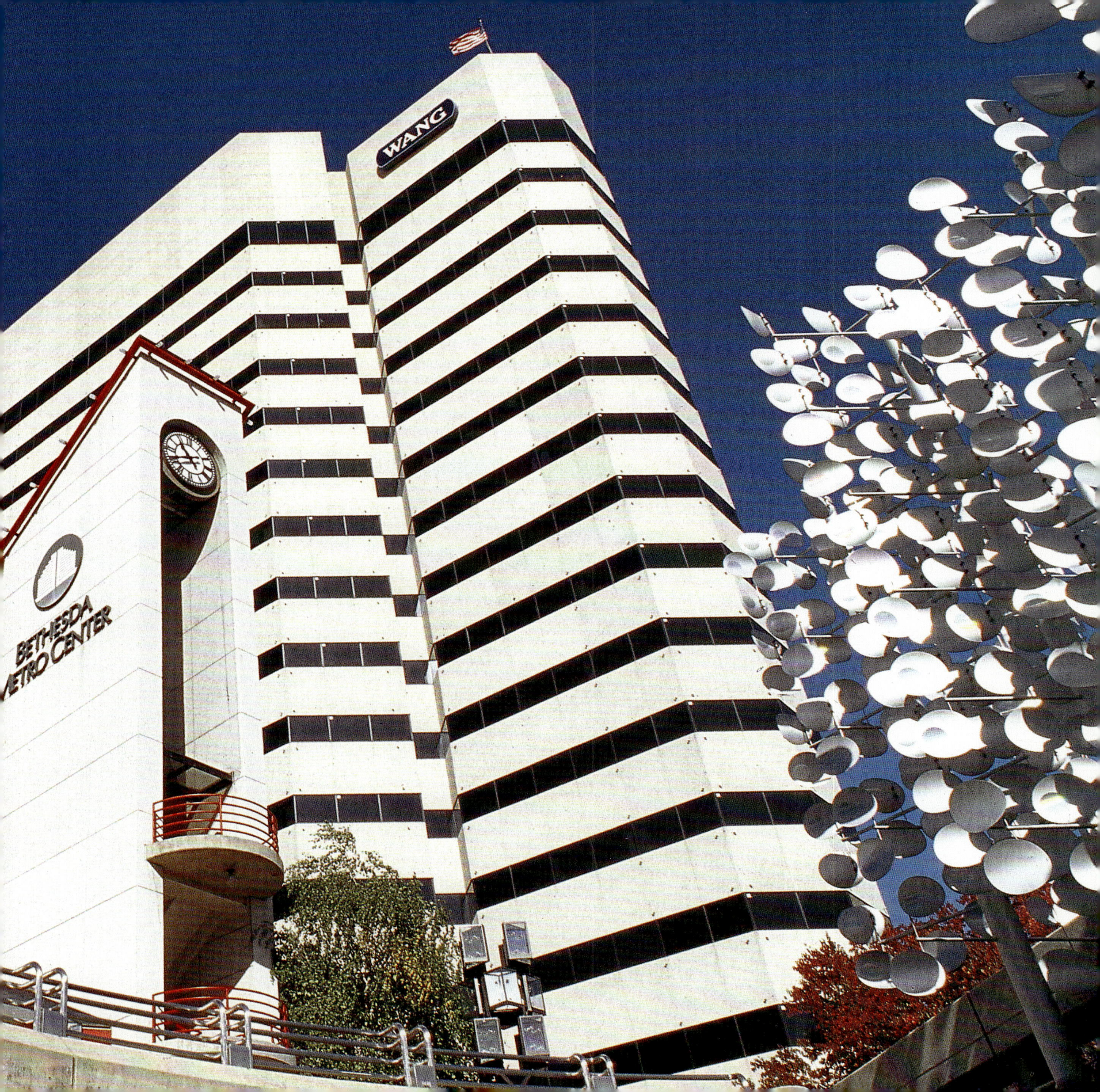
WANG
BETHESDA

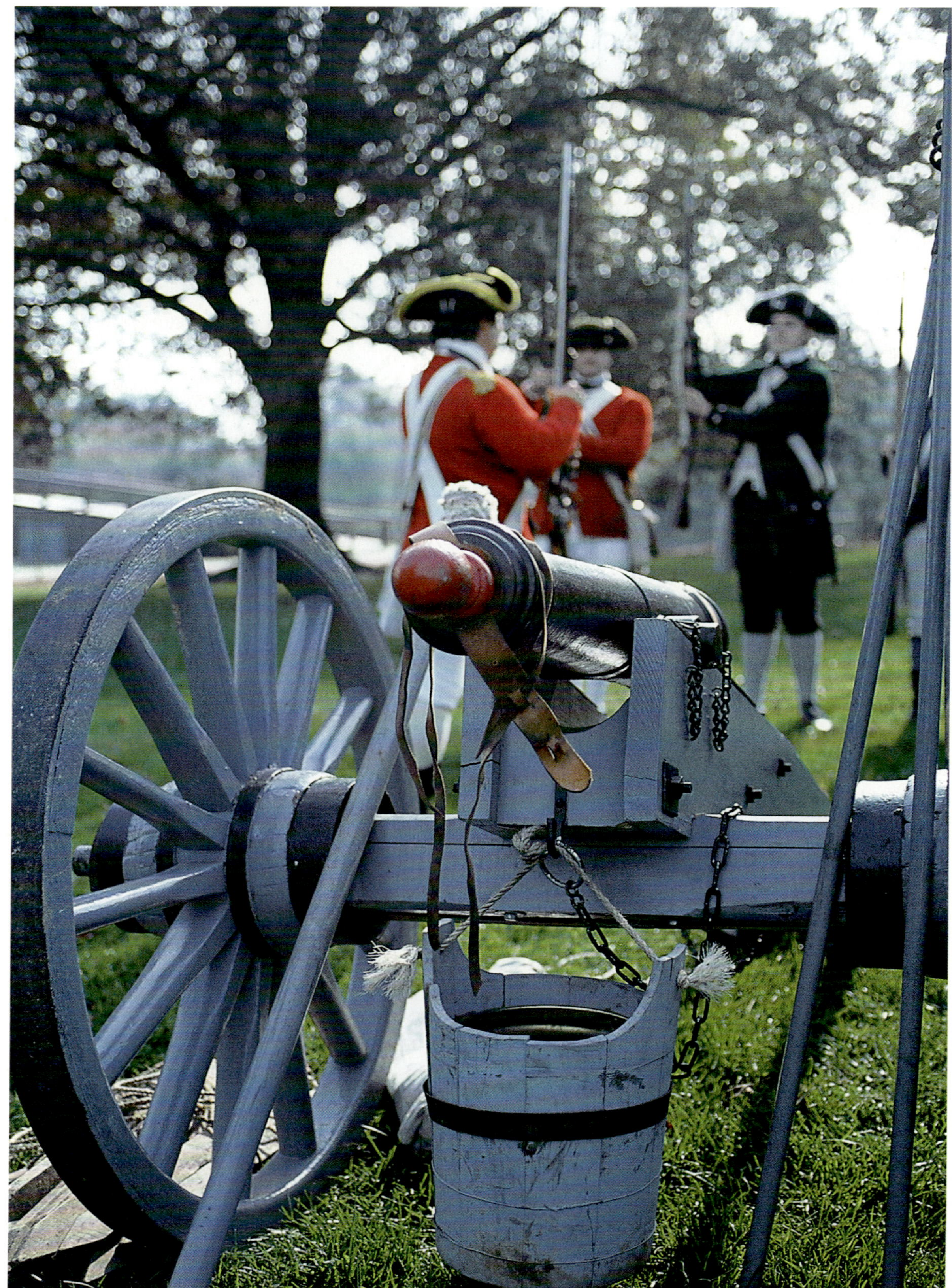

History buffs reenact a Revolutionary War battle in Montpelier, near Washington, D.C. While young men from the fledgling state joined the troops, many of Maryland's merchant vessels patroled the coast as makeshift warships.

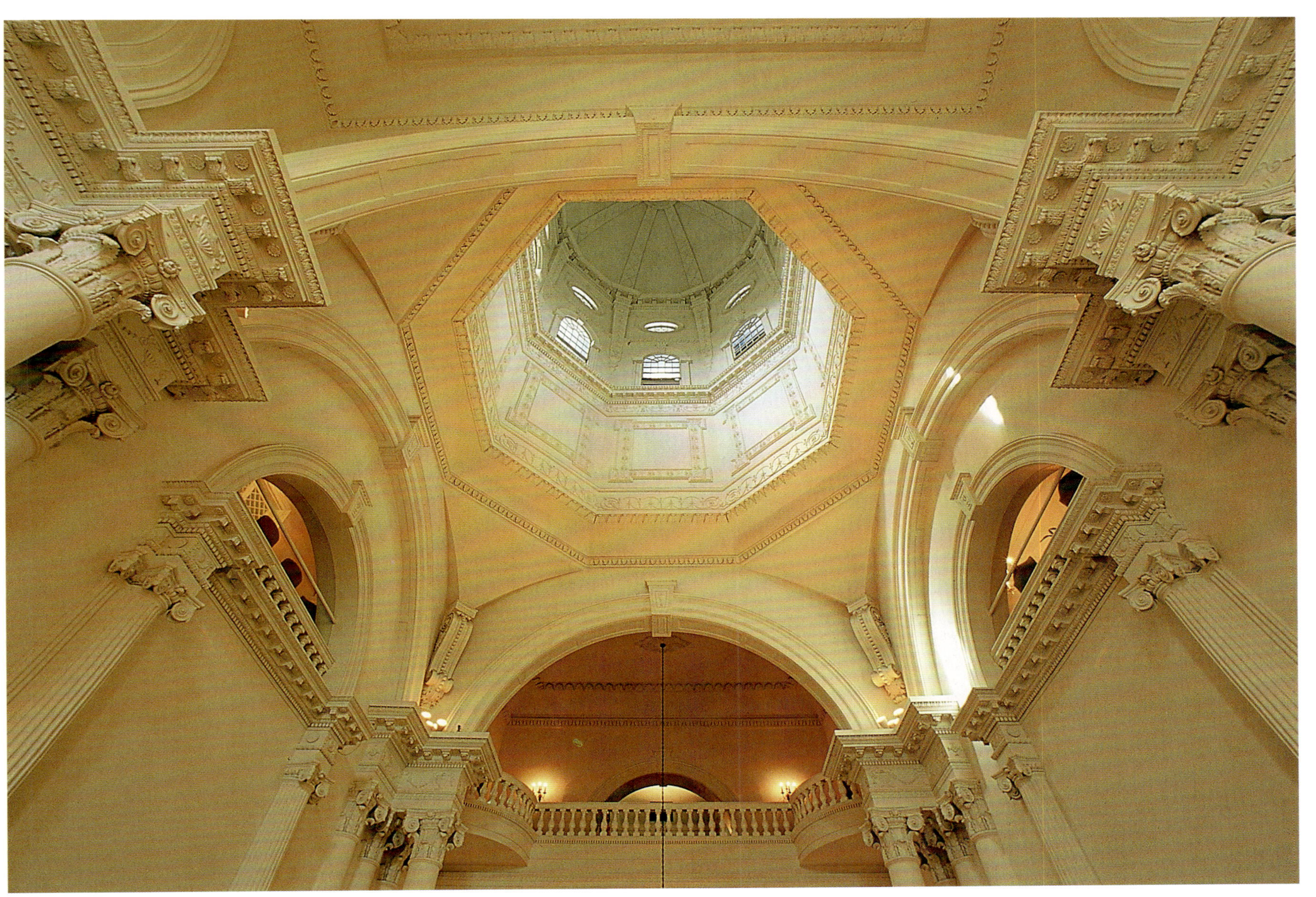

Joseph Horatio Anderson designed Maryland's State House and supervised the beginning of construction in 1772. Designated a national historic landmark, this is the oldest state house still in use by a state legislature.

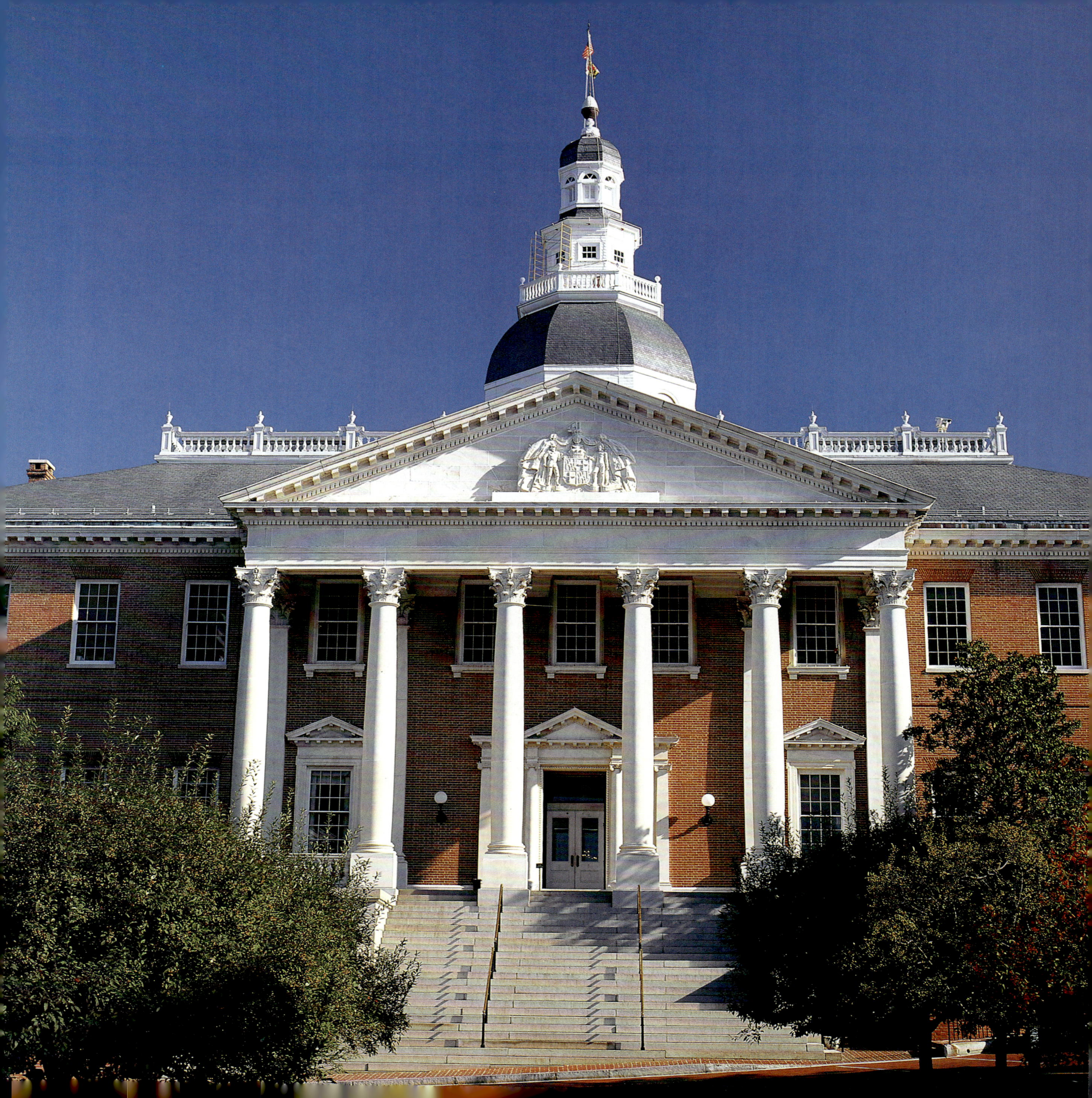

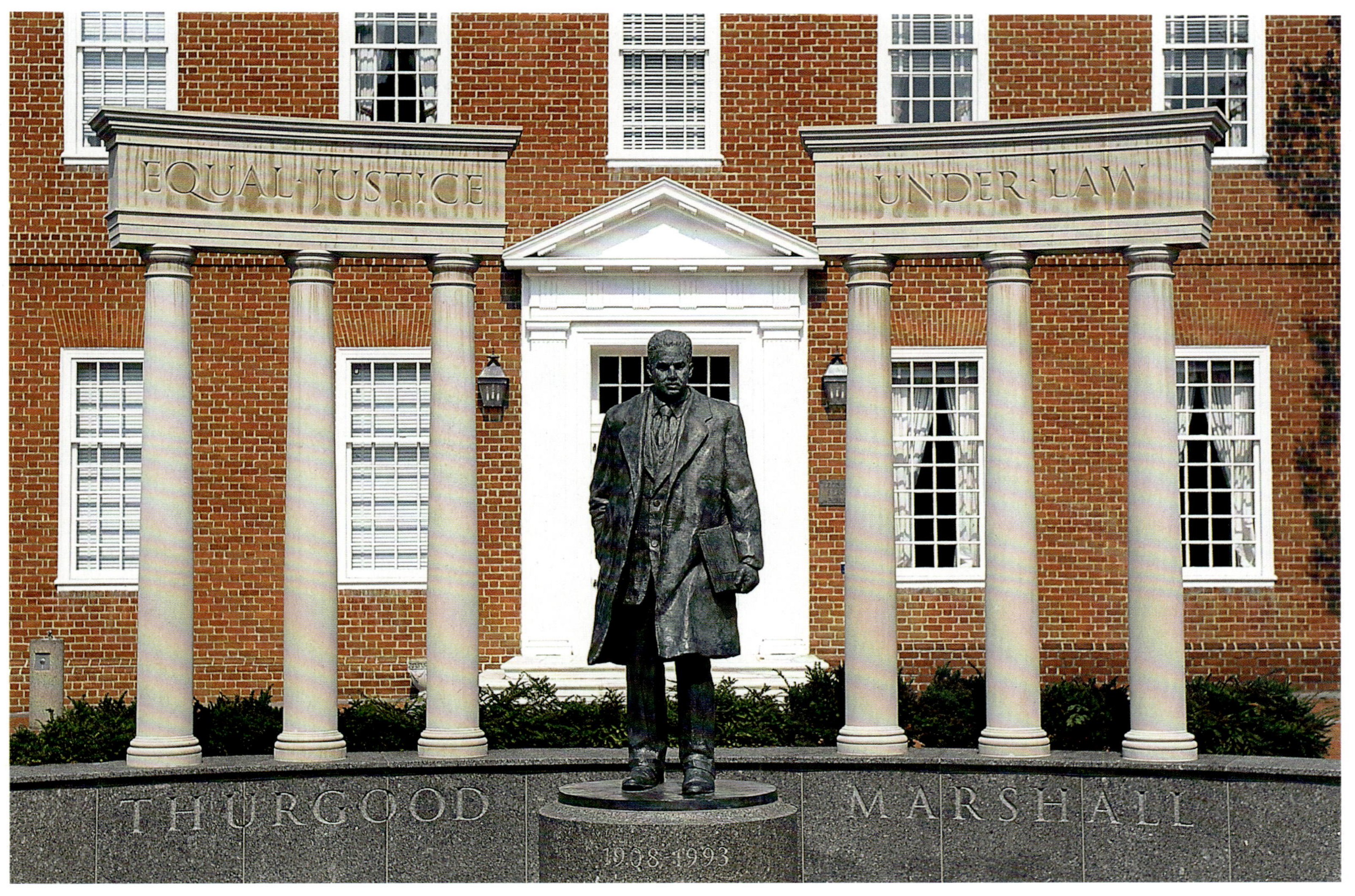

The Thurgood Marshall Memorial in Annapolis honors one of the leaders of America's civil rights movement. A lawyer and a Harvard graduate, Marshall dedicated much of his life to the National Association for the Advancement of Colored People. In 1967, he became the first African American to serve on the U.S. Supreme Court.

Atop Maryland's State House stands a 28-foot-tall lightning rod, built after consultation with Benjamin Franklin. For more than two centuries, the rod has protected the 113-foot-high wooden dome and the surrounding structure.

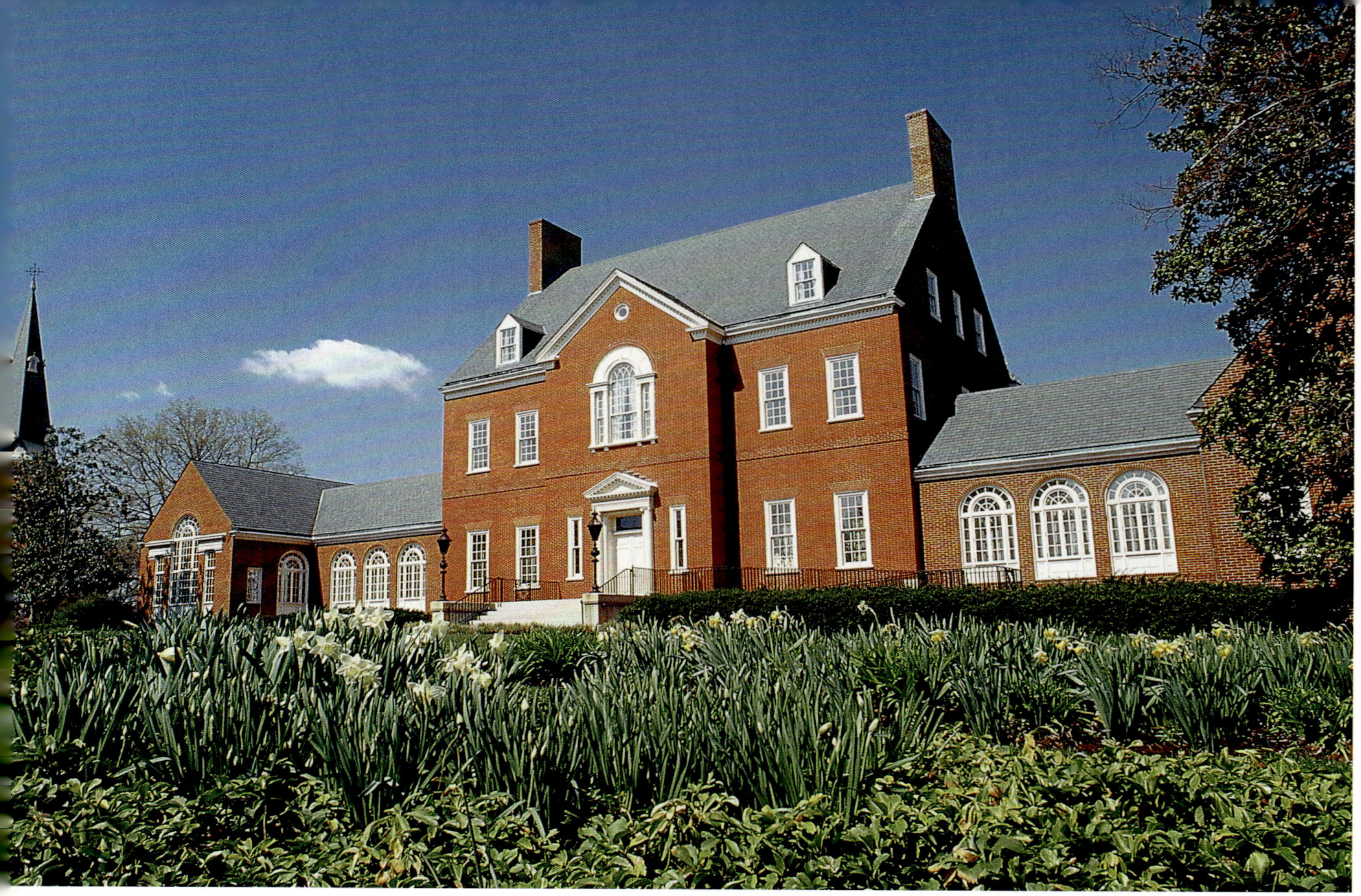

For more than 125 years, this Georgian mansion in Annapolis has been home to Maryland's governors. Visitors can tour seven public rooms within the home, including the Victorian library, the conservatory, and the parlor. Historic treasures and works by some of Maryland's most prominent artists are on display.

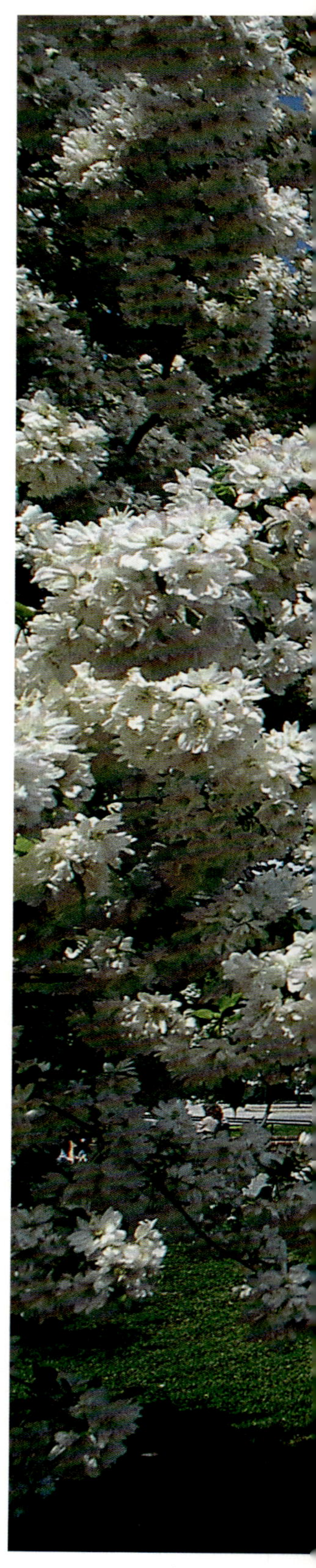

Blossoms frame the Legislative Services Building in Annapolis. Founded in 1649, the city was named for Princess Anne, the youngest daughter of King James II. Annapolis served as the capital of the region since 1694. From 1783 to 1784, during the Revolutionary War, Annapolis was also the capital of the newborn United States.

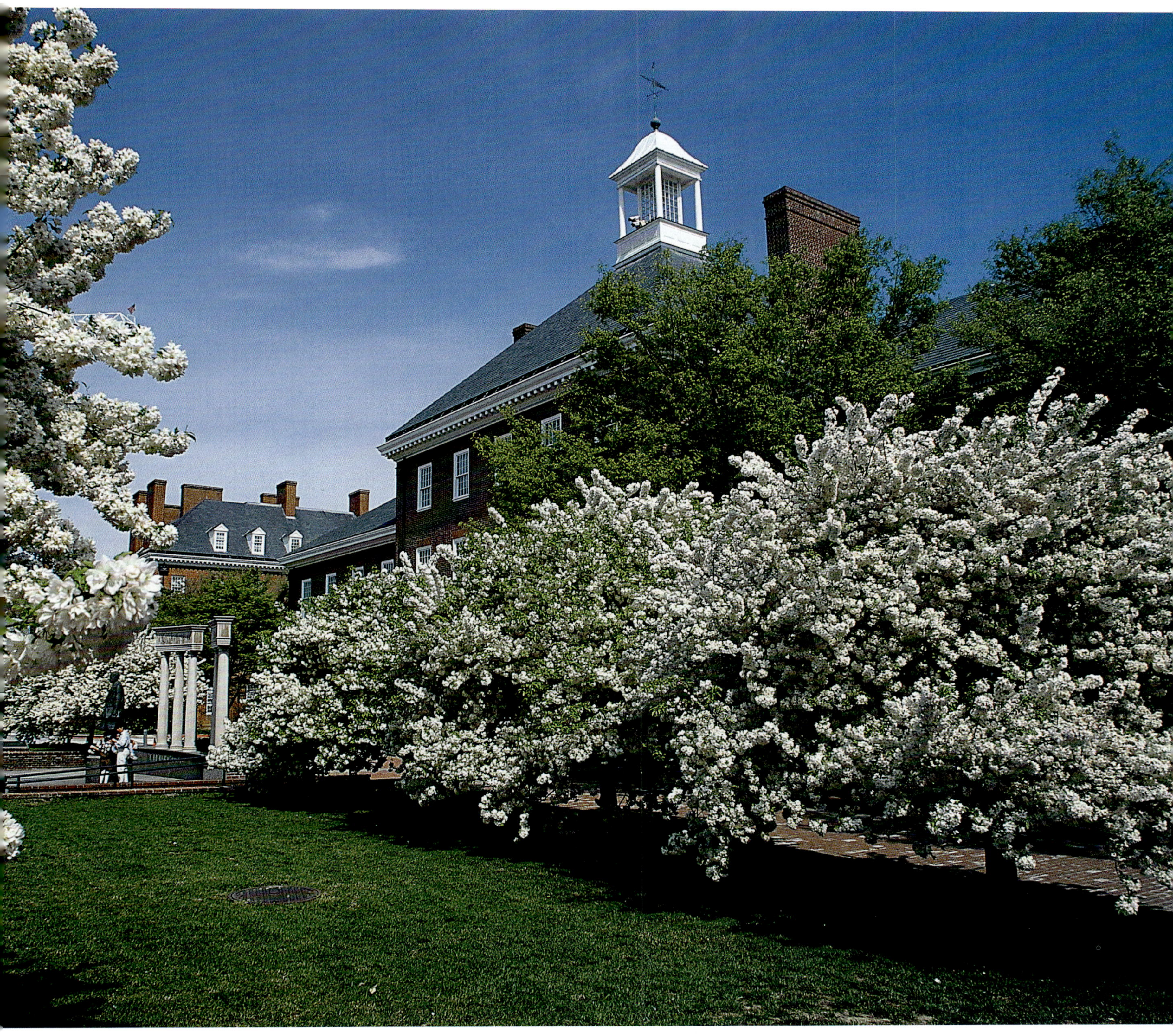

It's easy to imagine Annapolis as it was three centuries ago. In fact, visitors might spot a woman in petticoats or a man in knickers—most likely guides leading sightseers past some of the city's 1,500 historic buildings. Four Maryland leaders signed the Declaration of Independence, and each of their homes still stands within the city.

FACING PAGE
Annual boat shows and yacht races on Chesapeake Bay contribute to Annapolis's reputation as the Sailing Capital of the World. Formed at the end of the last ice age, when glacial meltwater flooded the Susquehanna River, Chesapeake Bay is 190 miles long, but only an average of 22 feet deep. The deepest channel reaches 174 feet.

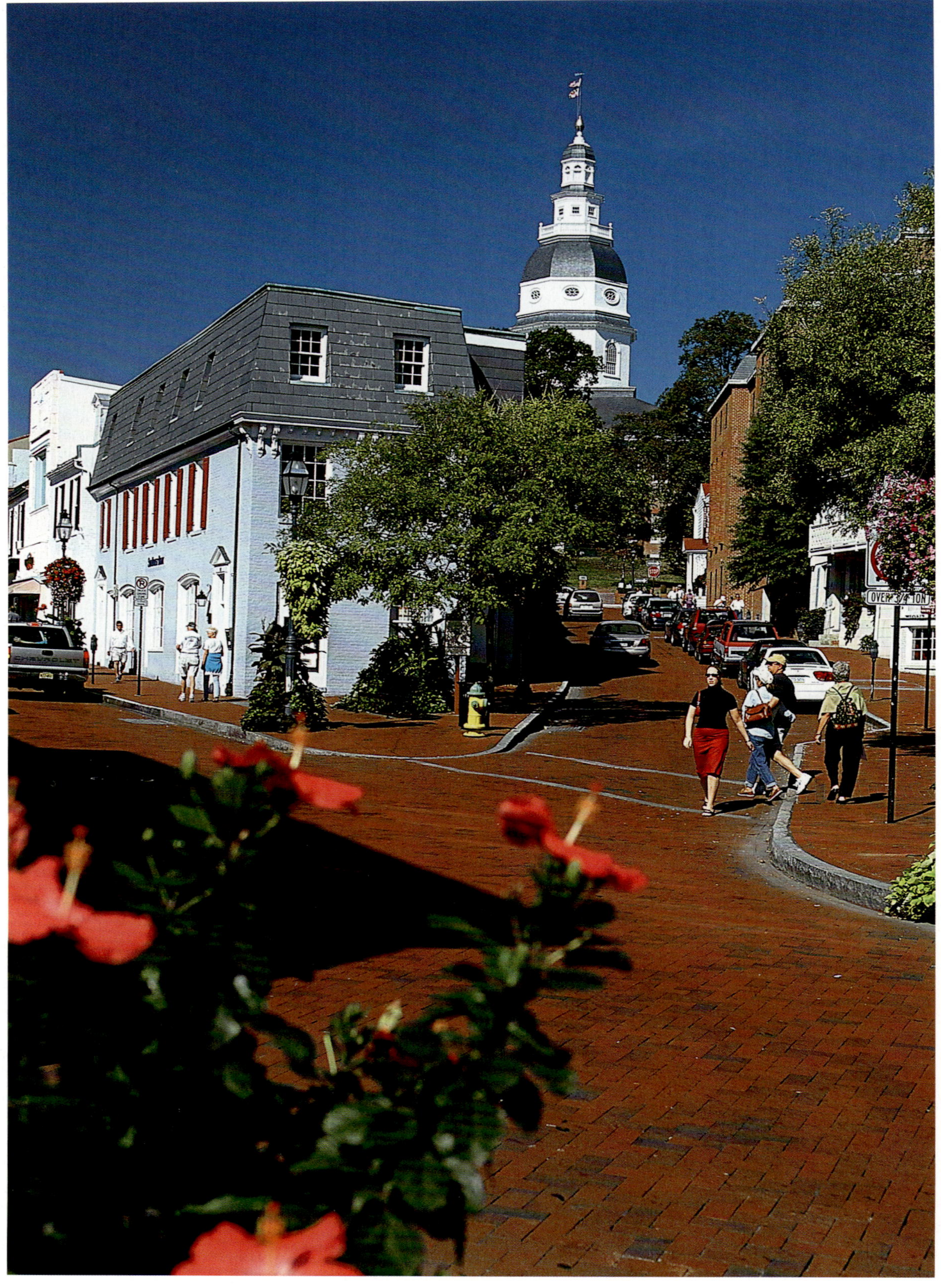

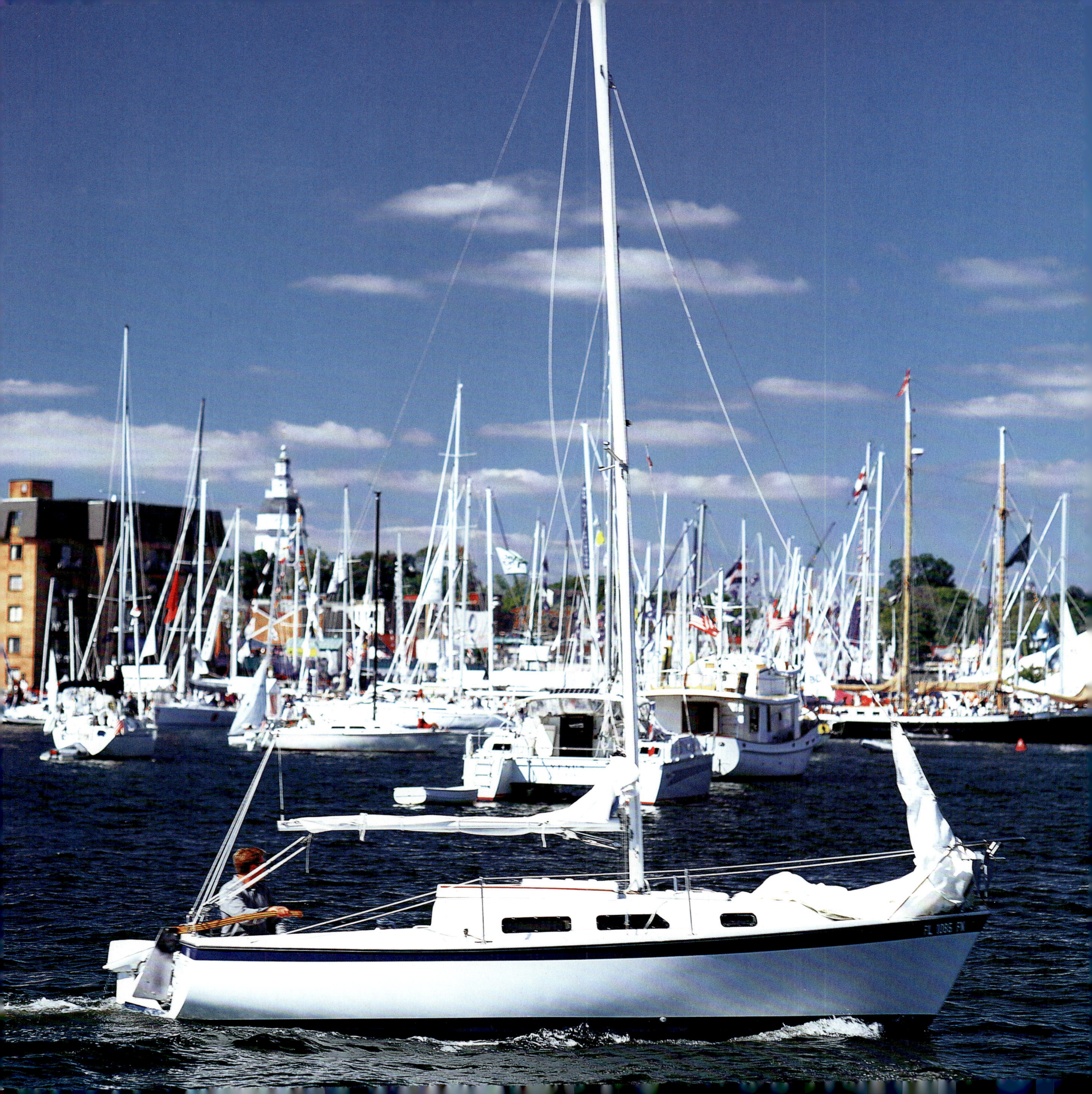

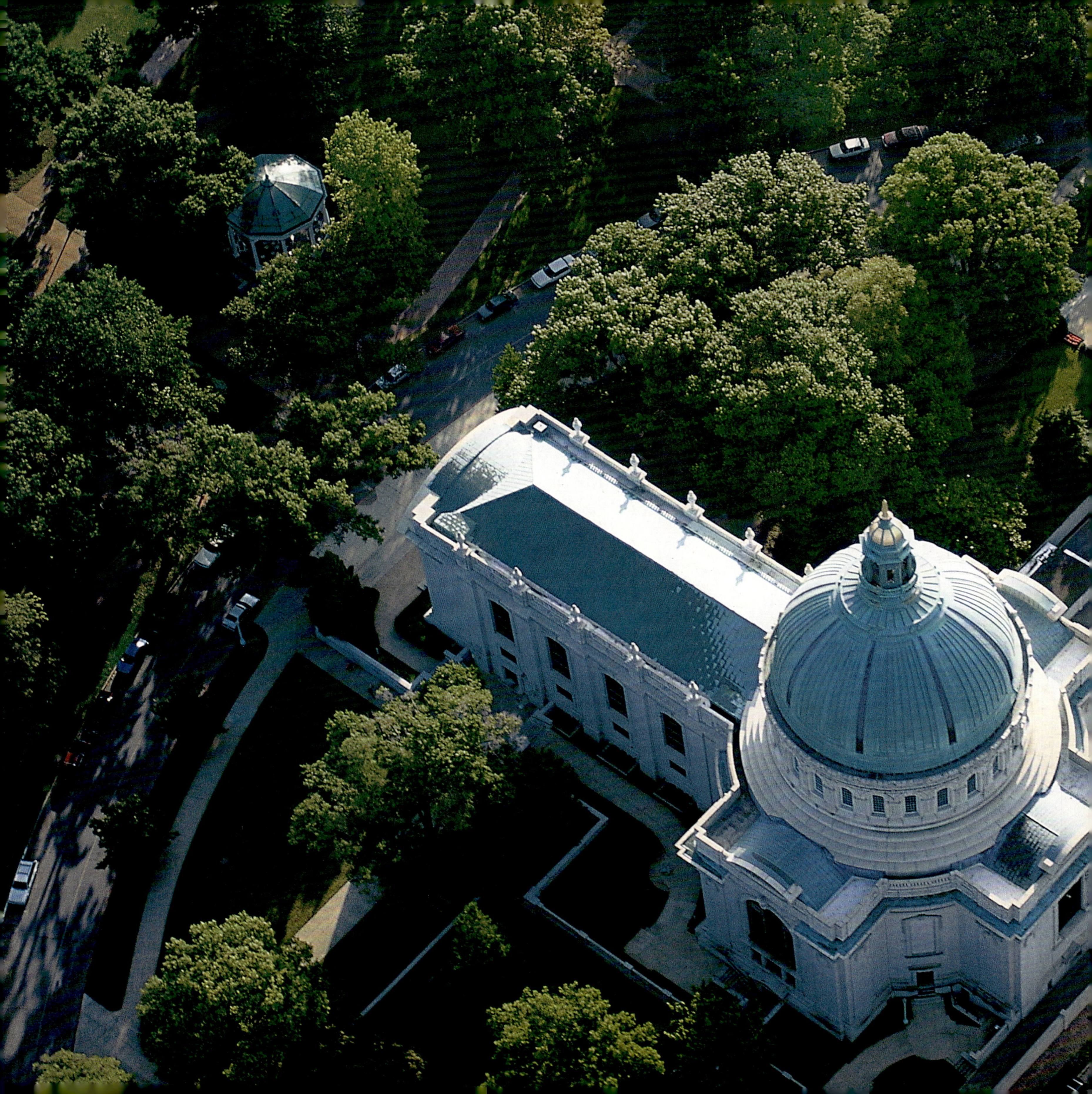

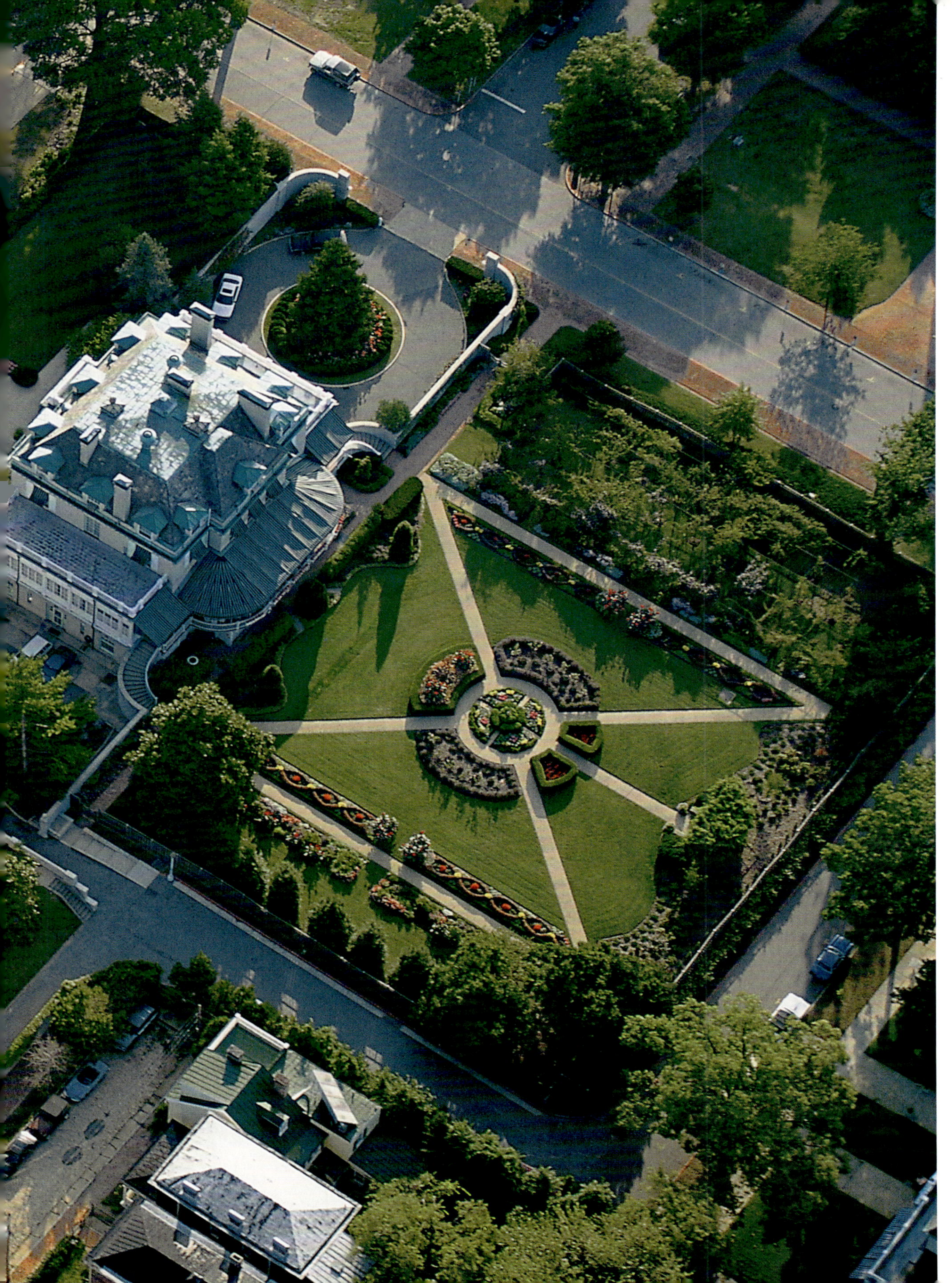

Since its establishment in 1845, more than 60,000 men and women have attended the U.S. Naval Academy in Annapolis, training to become officers in the U.S. Navy and Marine Corps. The four-year immersion program includes class-room lectures, practical training, and summers aboard navy vessels.

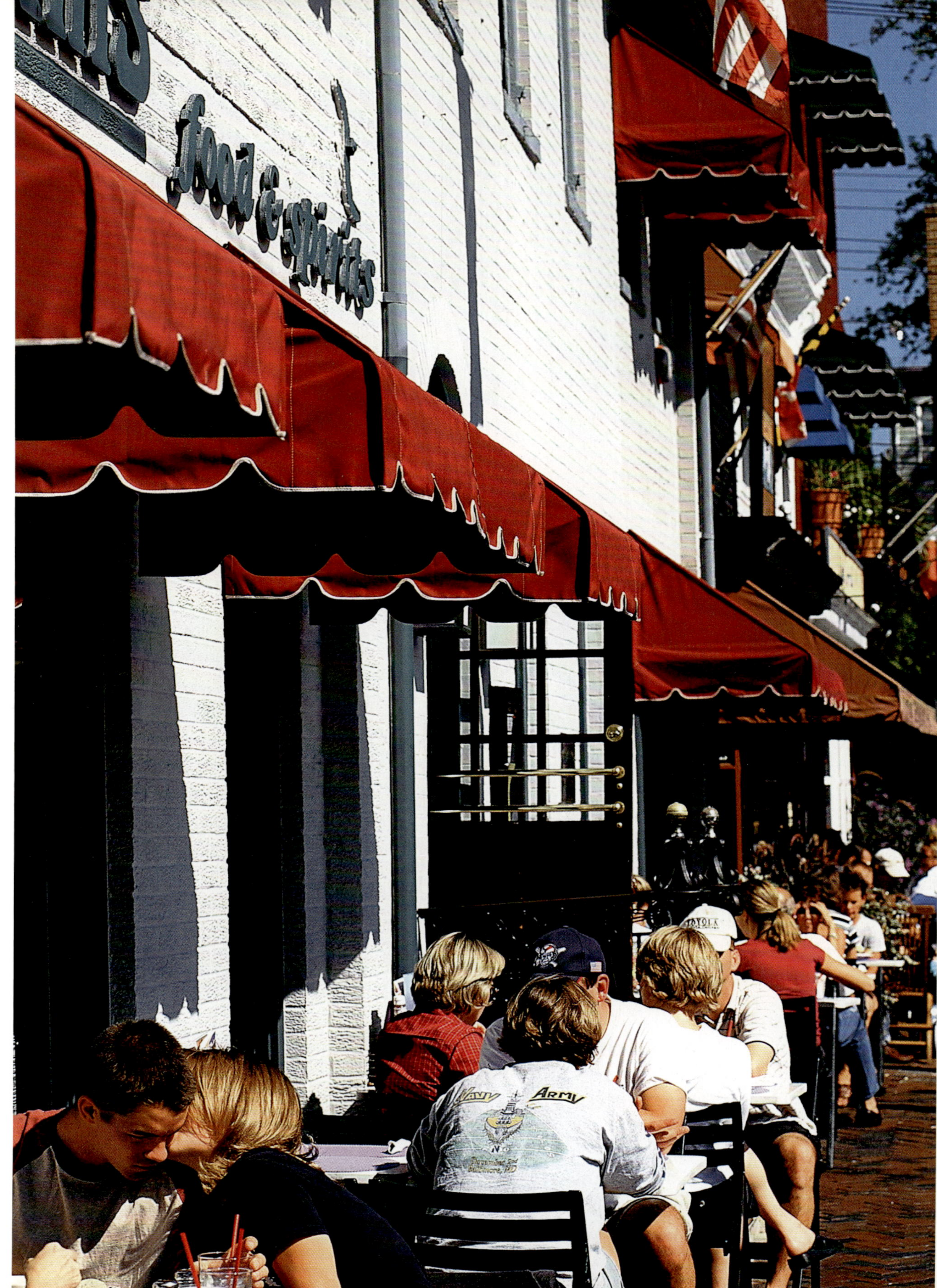

From seafood restaurants and colonial-style taverns to bay-side bistros and Italian eateries, Annapolis is the gourmand's ideal destination. Local specialties include crab cakes, stuffed rockfish, and black walnut pie.

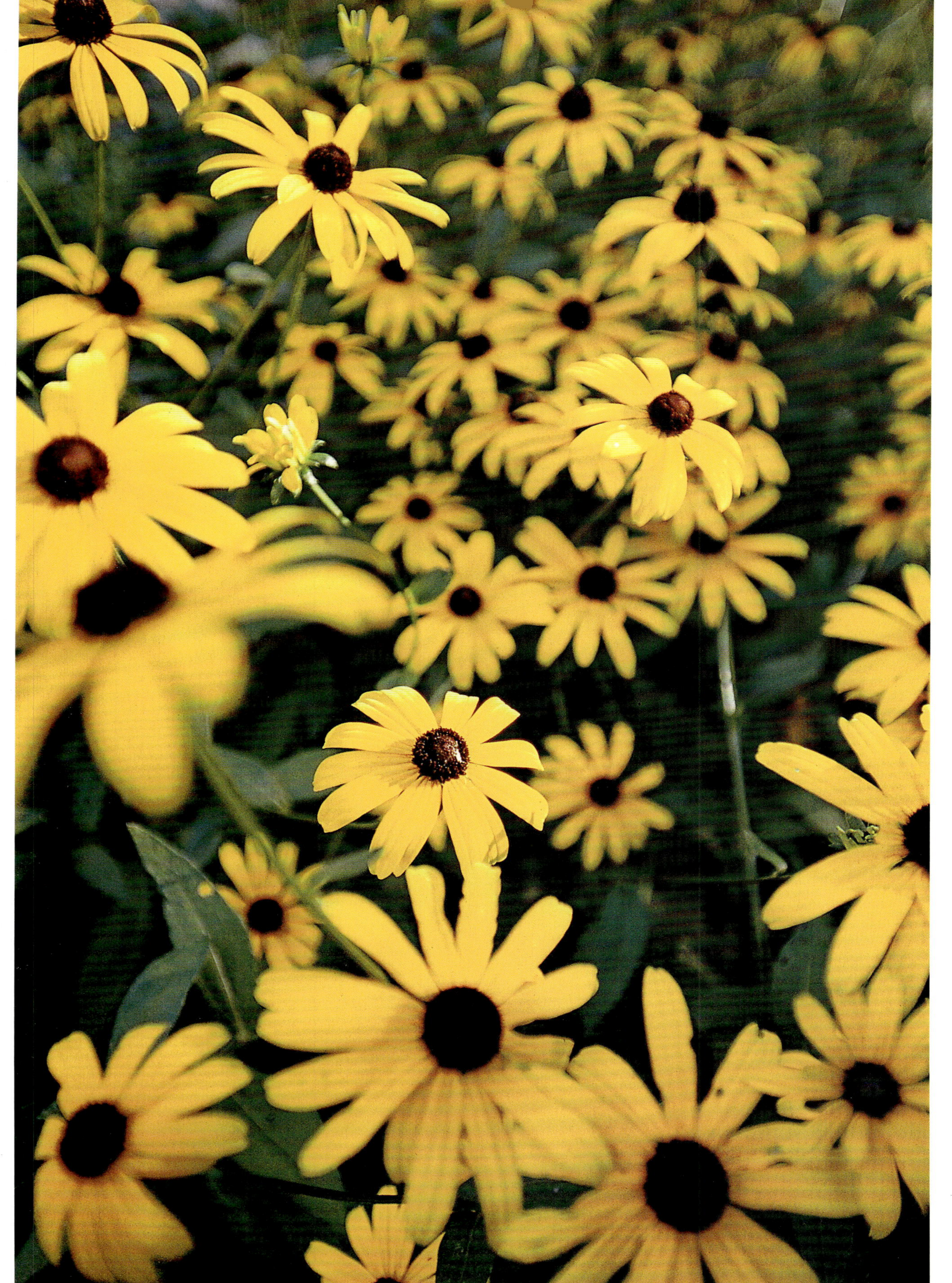

The state flower since 1918, black-eyed susans carpet meadows and fields from May until August. Other Maryland symbols include the Baltimore oriole, the Baltimore checkerspot butterfly, and the white oak. The blue crab is the state's official crustacean.

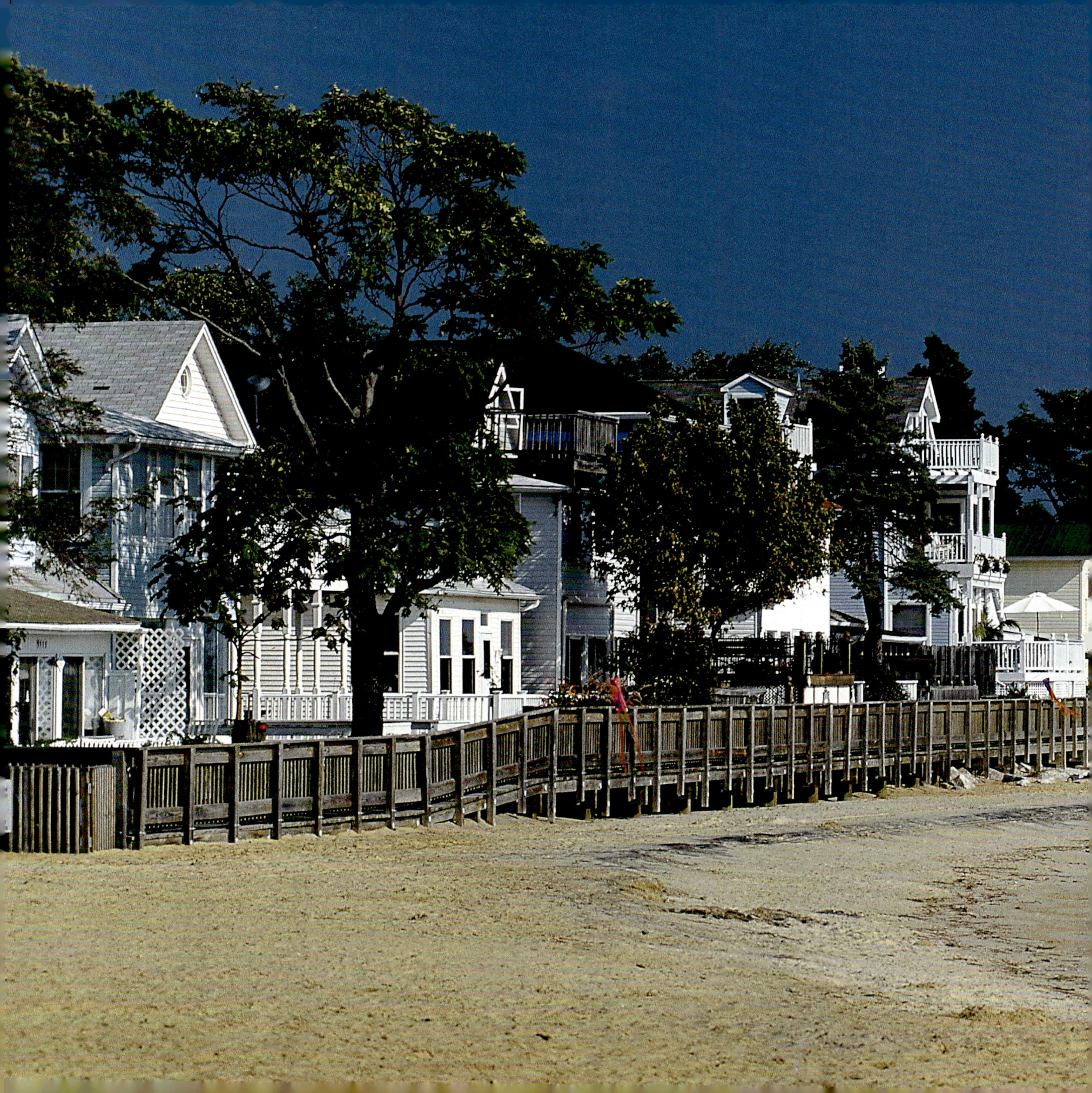

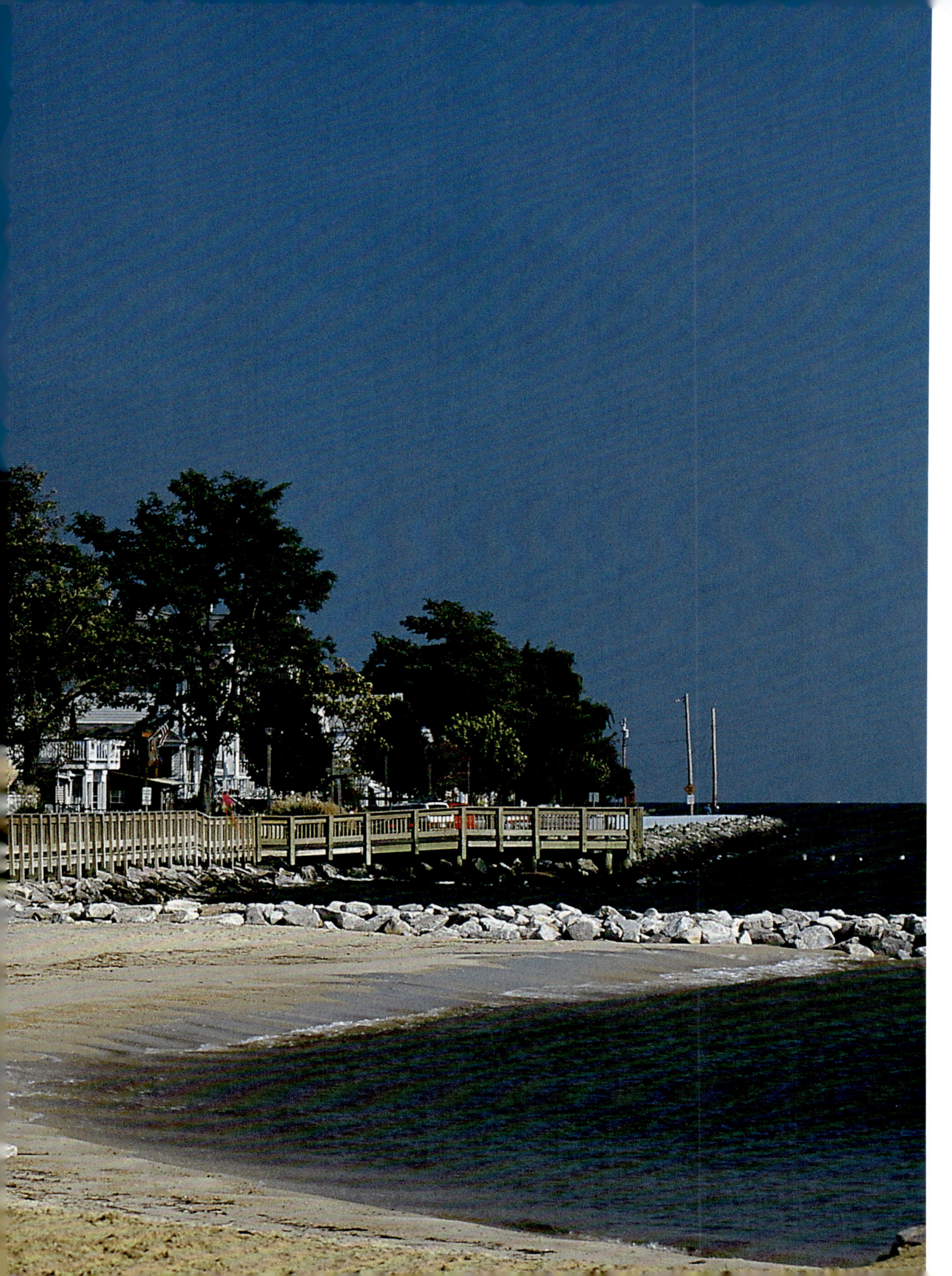

A boardwalk winds along the sands at North Beach, and a 550-foot pier offers the perfect place to fish or crab. Founded in 1900, North Beach originally served as a vacation retreat for Washington and Baltimore residents. Today the town has quaint cafés, antique shops, and an annual home and garden tour.

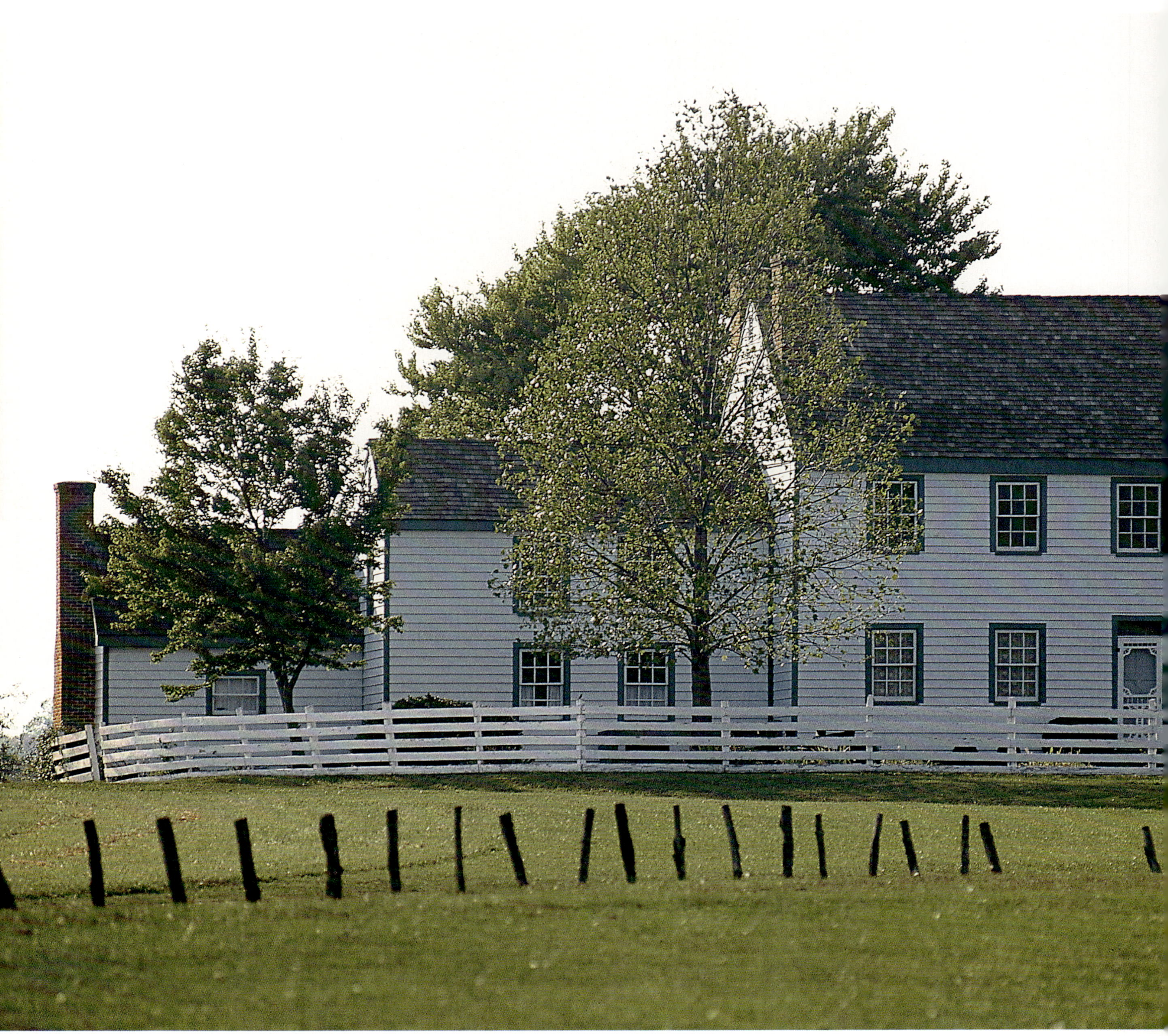

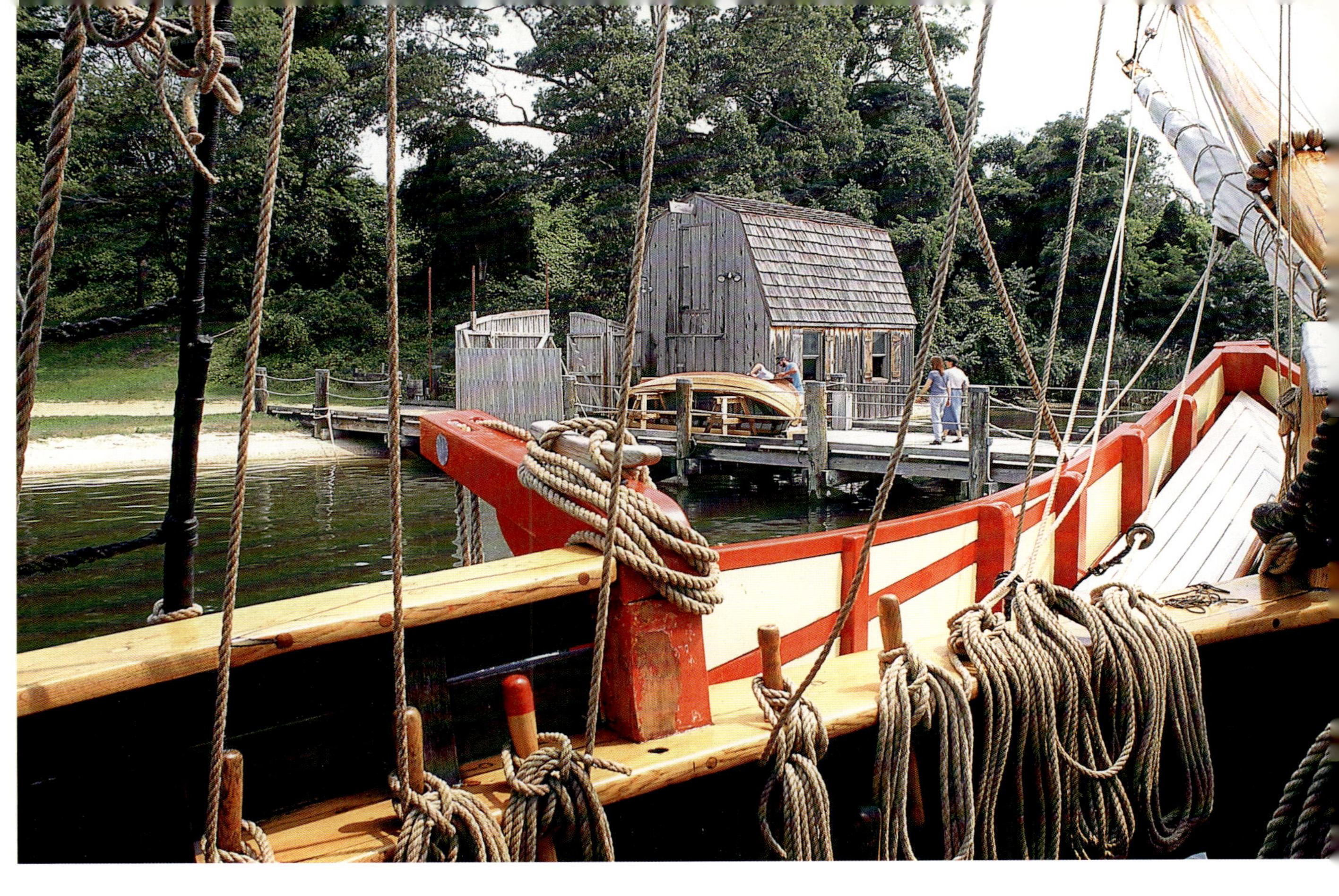

From this square-rigged ship, the *Maryland Dove*, to a reconstruction of a seventeenth-century inn, St. Mary's City provides visitors with a glimpse of the first permanent English colony in British North America. Led by Leonard Calvert, the settlers arrived in 1634 and quickly established a successful farming and fishing community.

The home of Dr. Samuel Mudd, near Waldorf, is now a museum. Accused of conspiring with John Wilkes Booth, who assassinated Abraham Lincoln in 1865, Mudd received a life sentence. The doctor maintained that he had simply set Wilkes's broken leg when the man arrived at his house in the middle of the night. Mudd was later pardoned by President Andrew Johnson.

This elegant home graces the Godiah Spray Tobacco Plantation in St. Mary's City. Here, costumed staff reenact the life of the Spray family. Planing wood for furniture, gathering medicinal herbs, tending the tobacco crop—the chores of 1661 are re-created daily.

FACING PAGE
Built in 1828, Cove Point Lighthouse marks a shoal that extends into a shipping lane on Chesapeake Bay. The structure next door housed two keepers and their families until the beacon was automated in 1986. Visible for 12 miles, its light continues to serve mariners today.

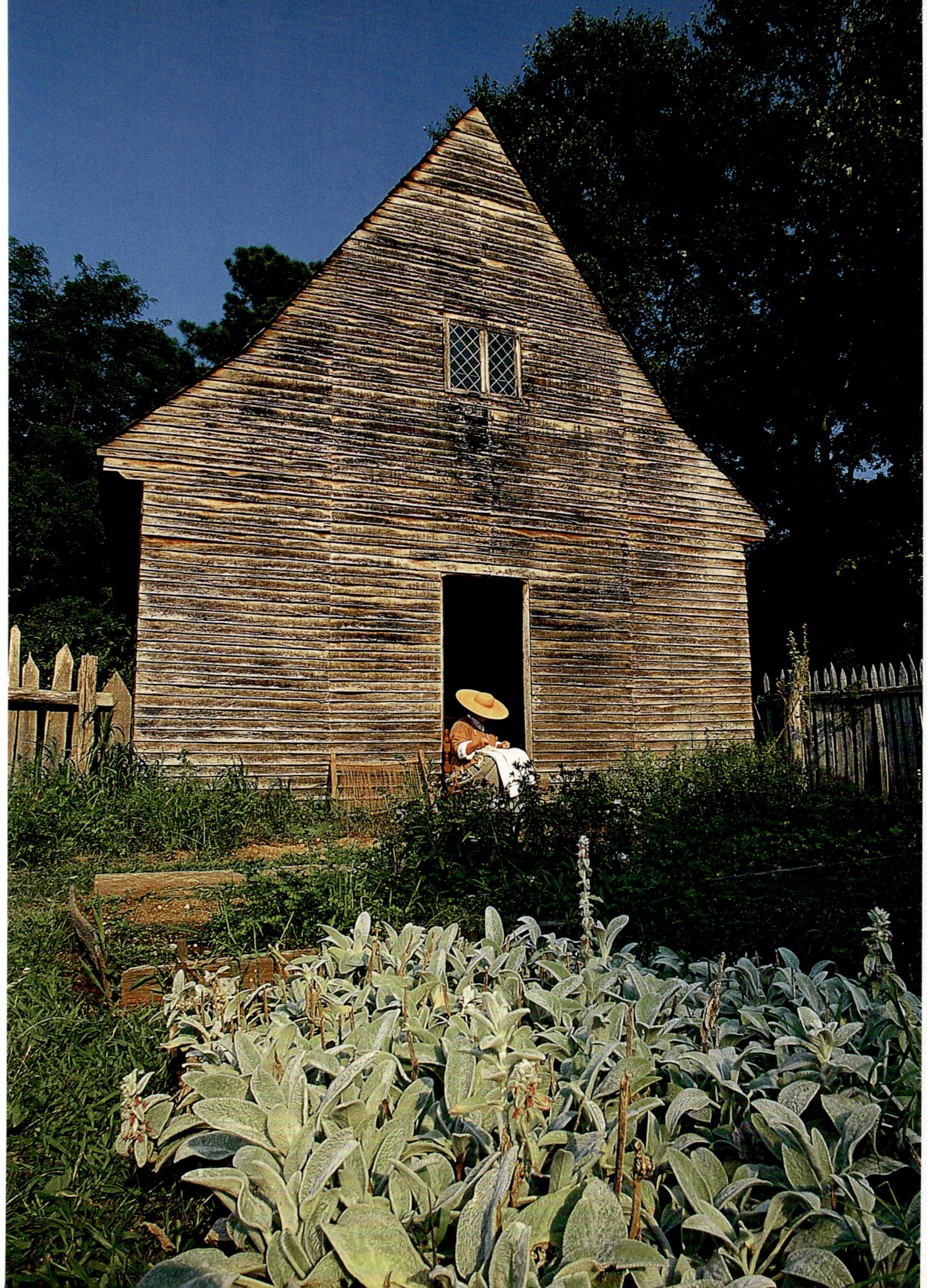

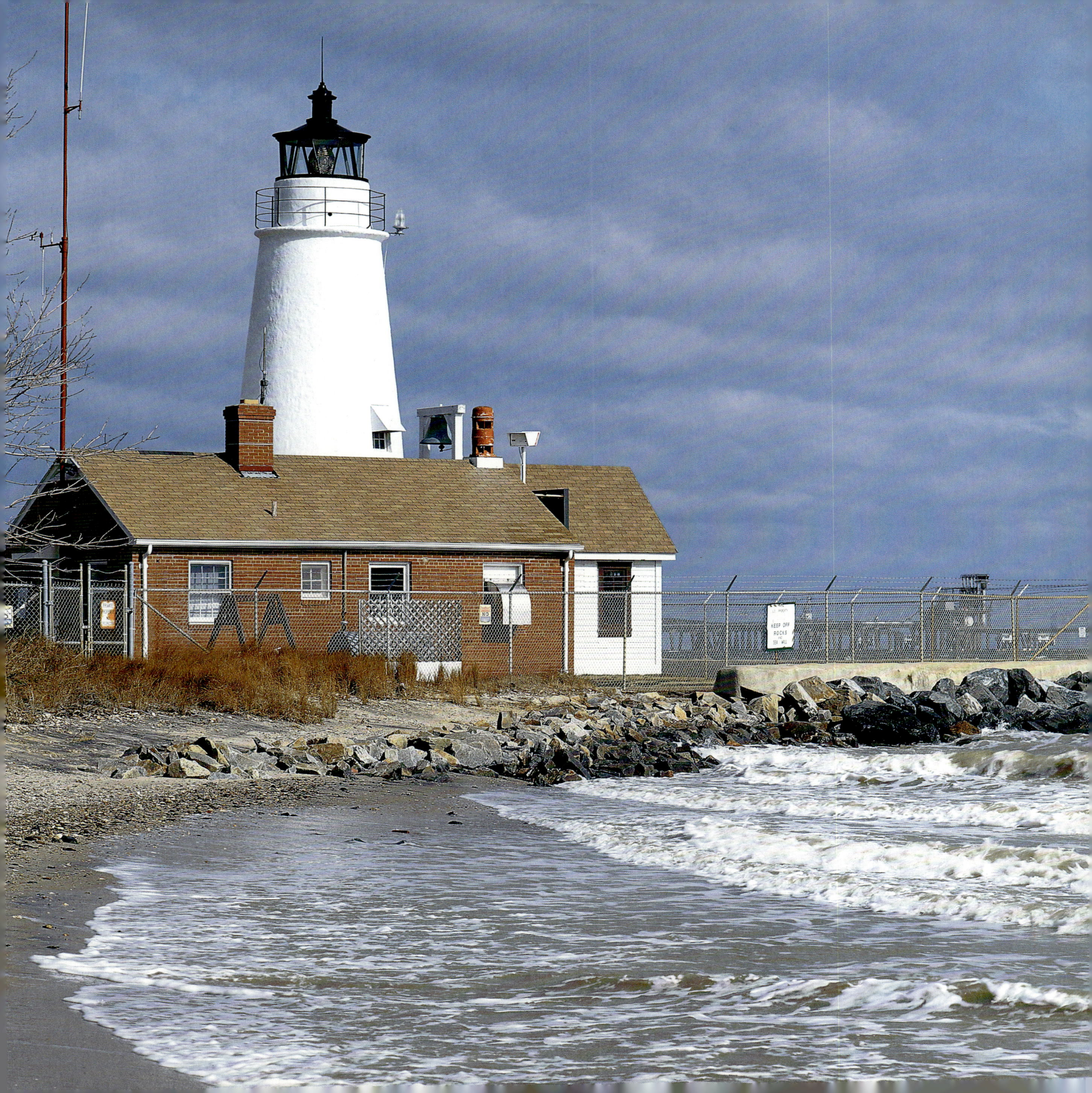
KEEP OFF
ROCKS
SEA WALL

Washington College in Chestertown is a four-year liberal arts college named for its first patron, George Washington. The central building shown here is named for William Smith, the president of the school when it opened in 1782. More than 1,200 students now attend classes here.

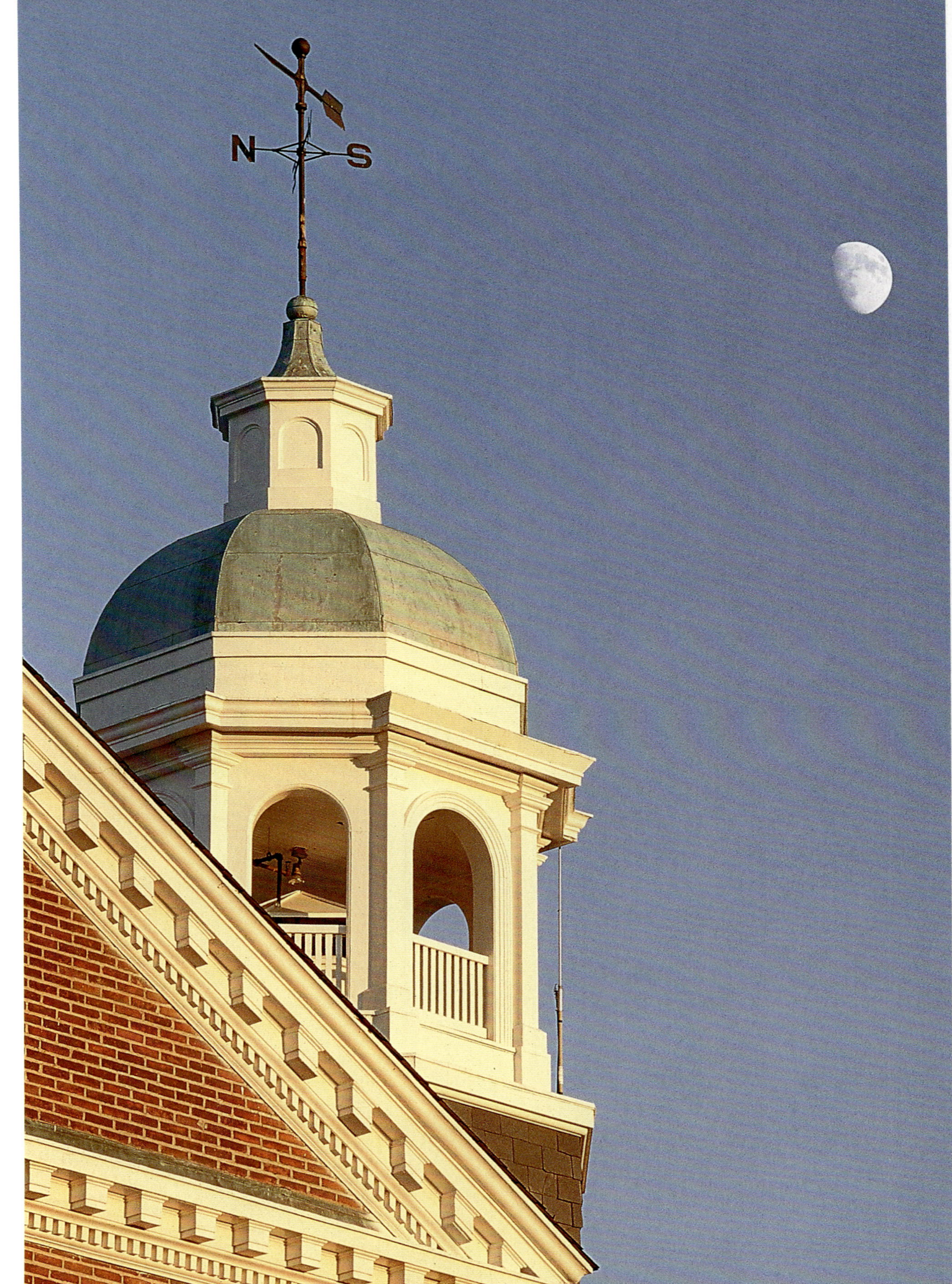

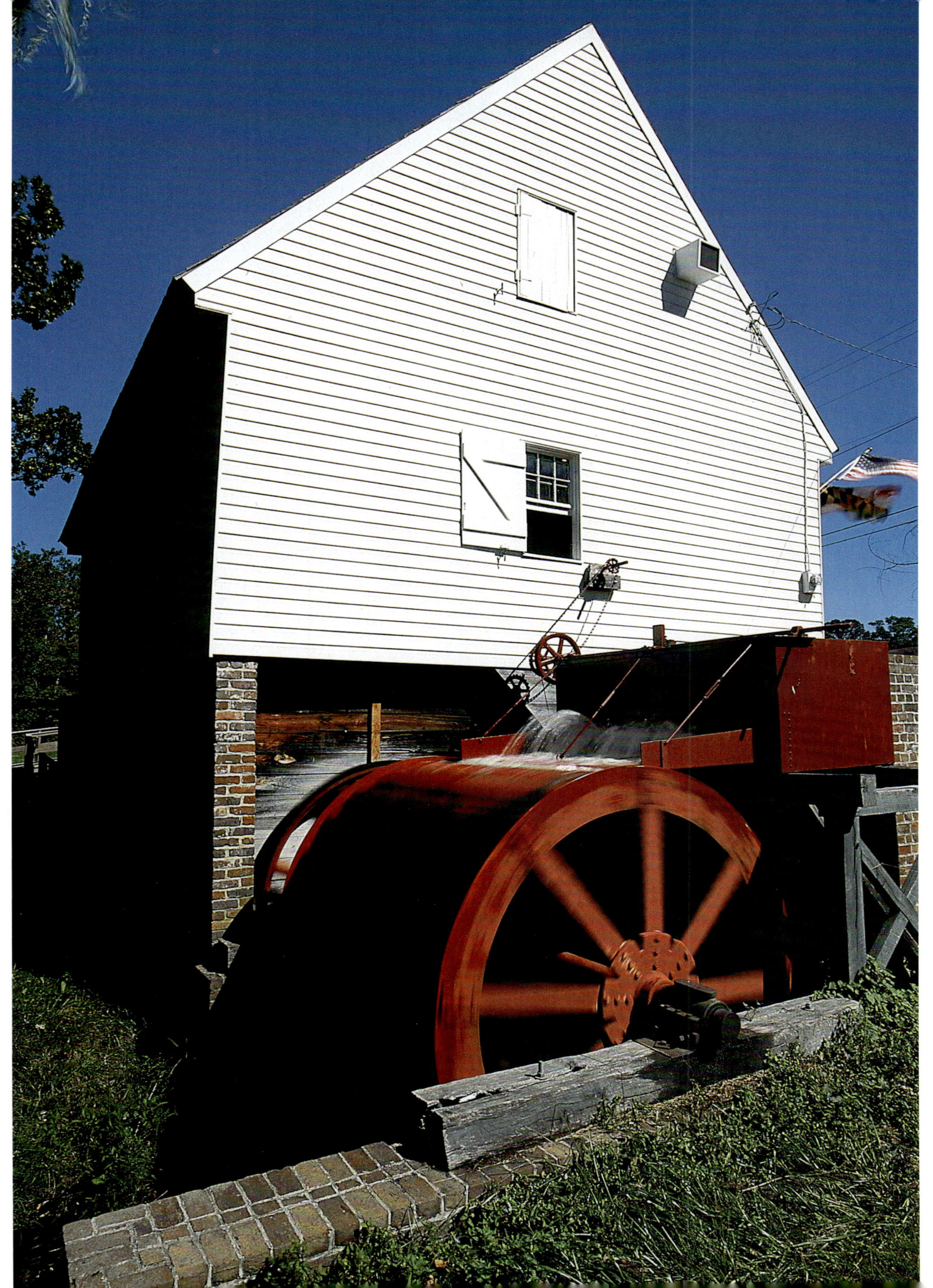

Throughout the seventeenth and eighteenth centuries, farmers from the Easton area brought their wheat and corn to Wye Grist Mill, where water power turned massive grinding stones, producing flour and meal. Today's mill looks much as it did in the early 1790s and springs to life twice each month when volunteers demonstrate its capabilities.

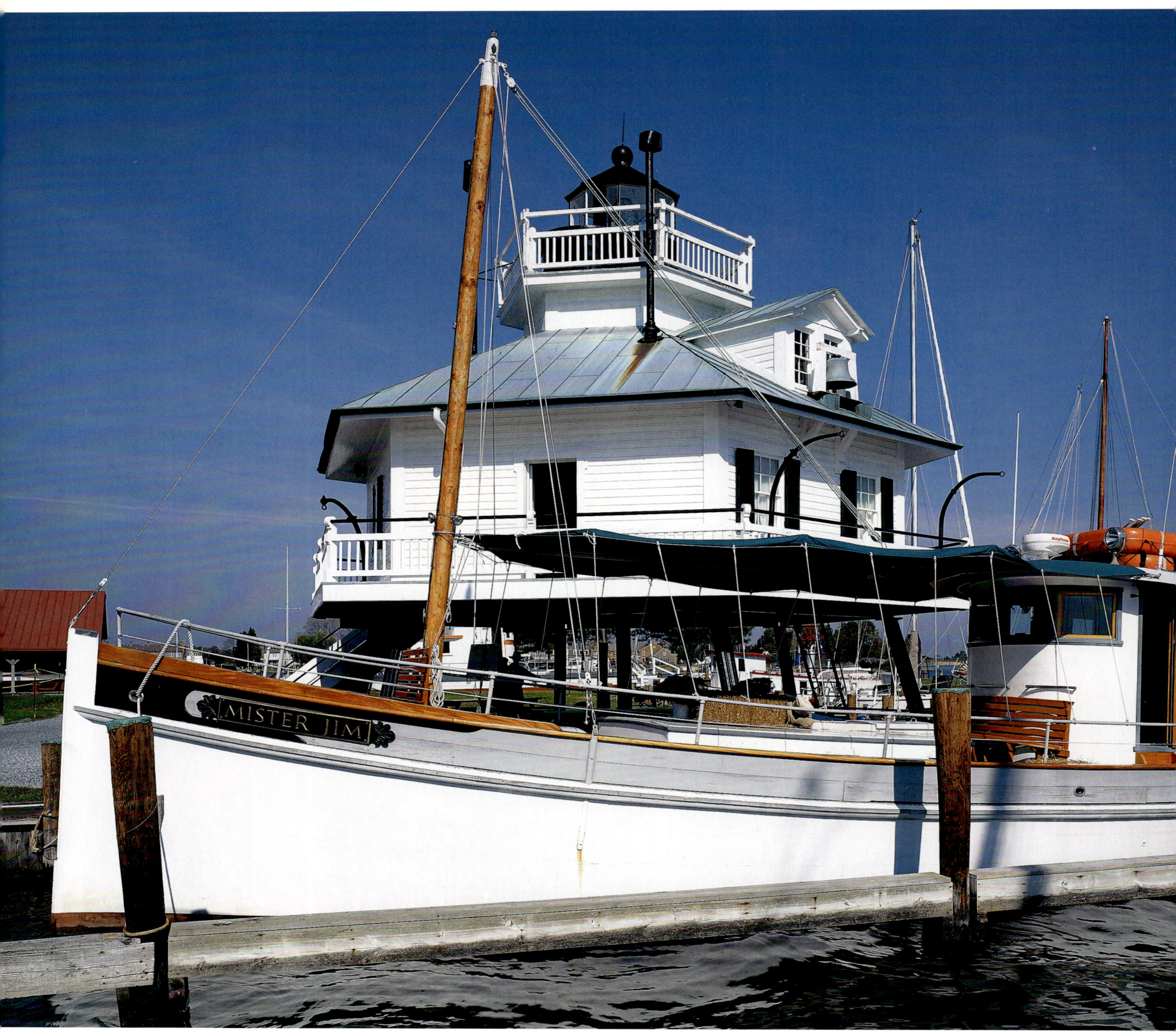
MISTER JIM

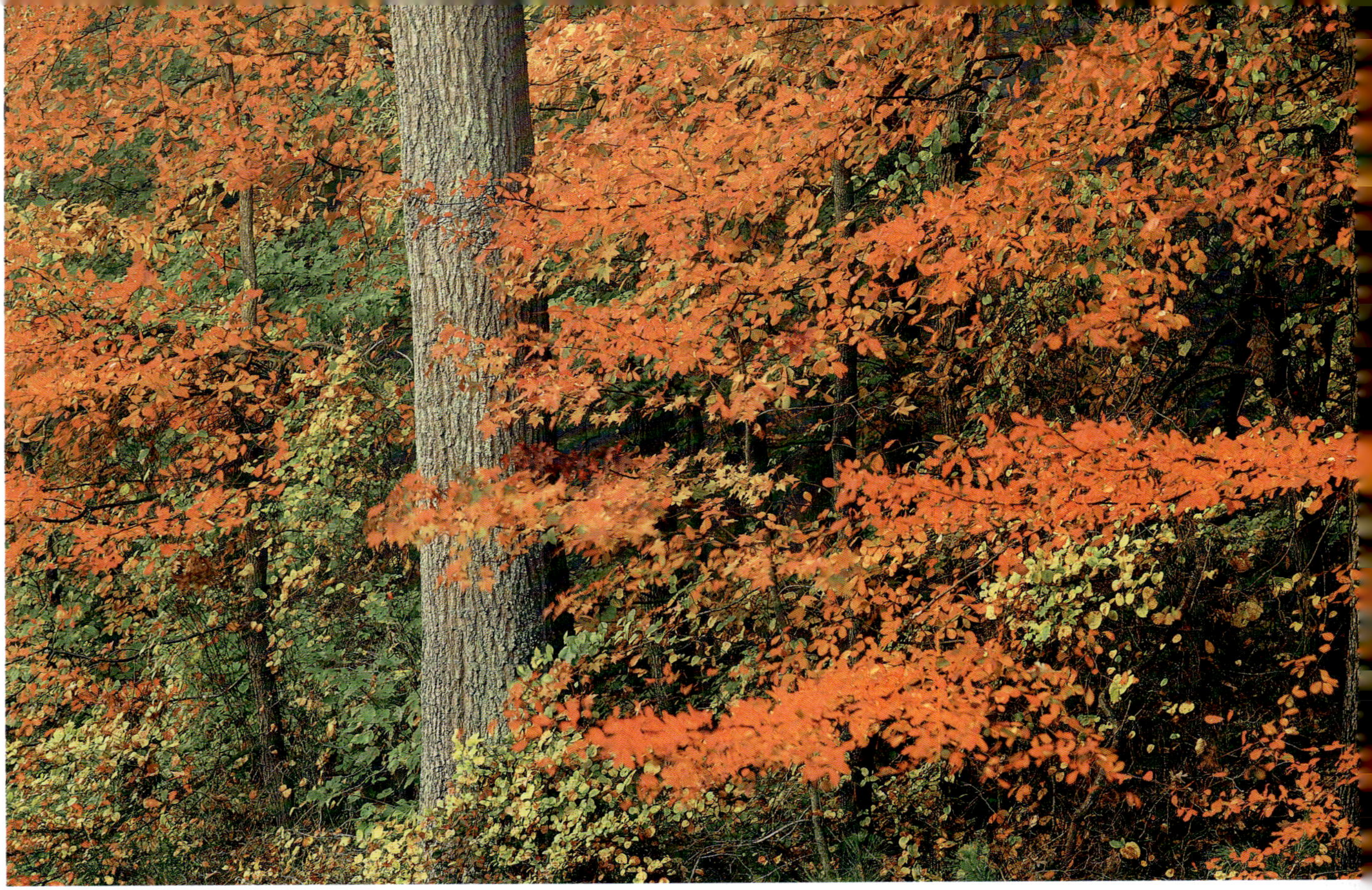

Kent Island is the largest island in Chesapeake Bay and once served as a trading post for Maryland's early settlers. With the construction of the Chesapeake Bay Bridge across the narrows in the 1950s, the island was suddenly accessible to visitors from Annapolis, Baltimore, and Washington. The beaches, marinas, quaint inns and historic sights continue to attract visitors today.

Through a working boatyard, a waterman's shanty, a seaside resort bandstand, and the refurbished 1879 Hooper Strait Lighthouse, the Chesapeake Bay Maritime Museum explores four centuries of history along the shores of the bay. The screwpile-style lighthouse stands on iron pilings, once used to anchor the structure in the soft sands of the shoreline.

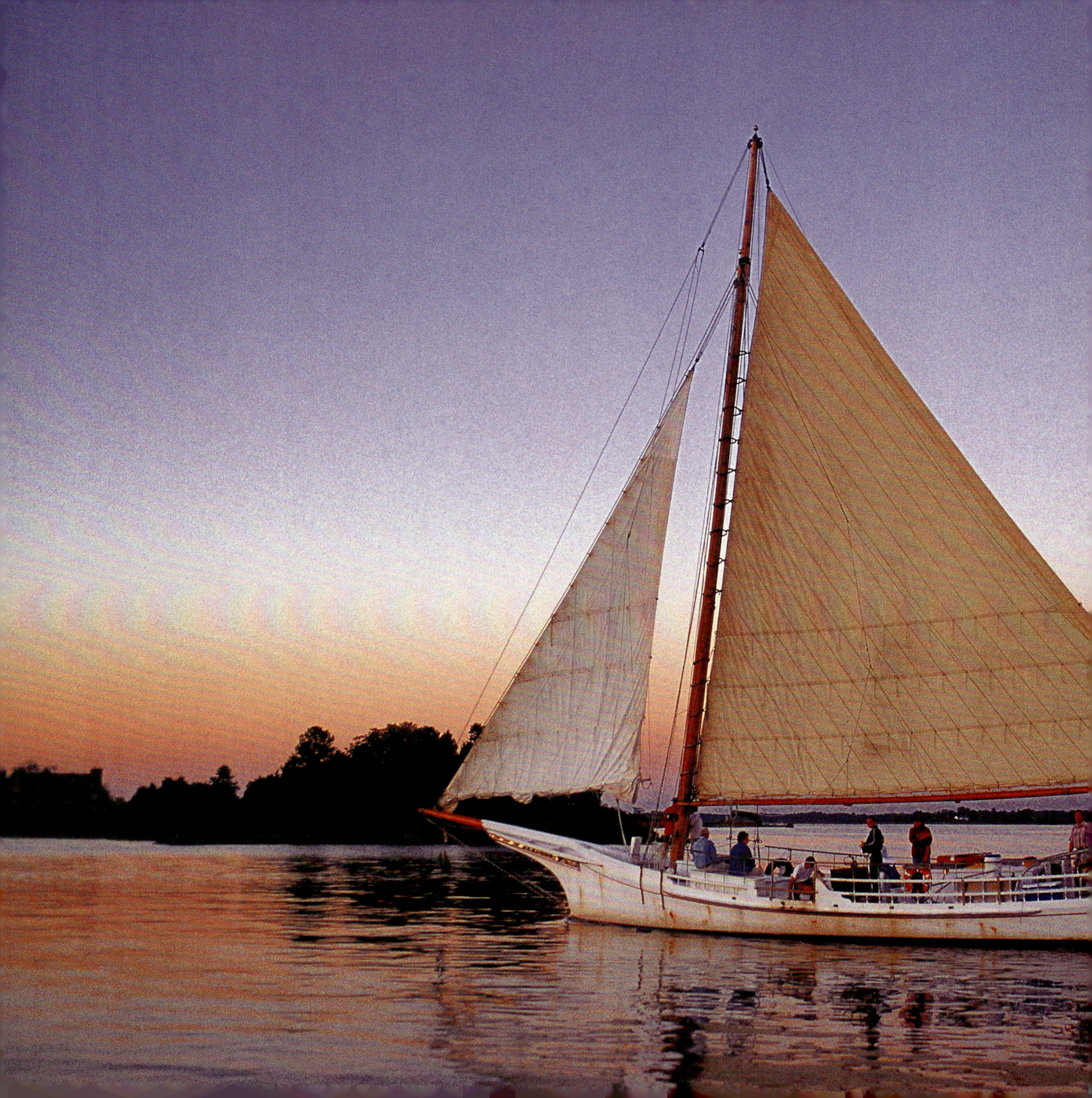

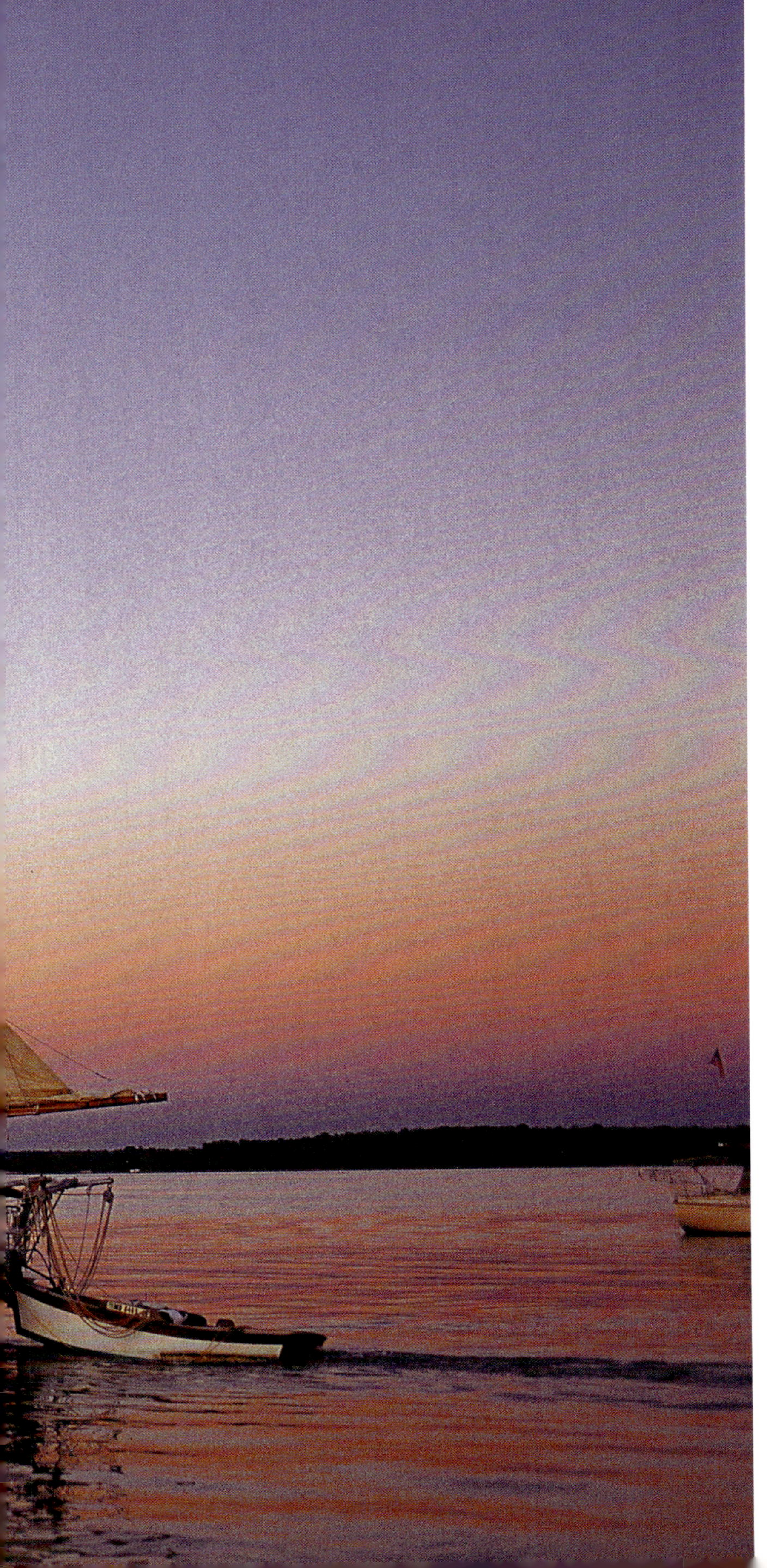

Named after leaping fish, such as skipjack herring or skipjack tuna, Maryland's skipjack oyster boats were the last American commercial vessels to work under sail. In the mid-1900s, more than 80 boats crisscrossed Chesapeake Bay, dredging shellfish from oyster beds on the bay's floor.

OVERLEAF
For centuries, shipbuilders in St. Michaels plied their trade along the shore while farmers tended tobacco and wheat just a few miles inland. According to local legend, the British attacked St. Michaels in 1813. The canny residents tricked the invading ships by darkening their homes and rigging new "harbor lights" on trees and masts a short distance away.

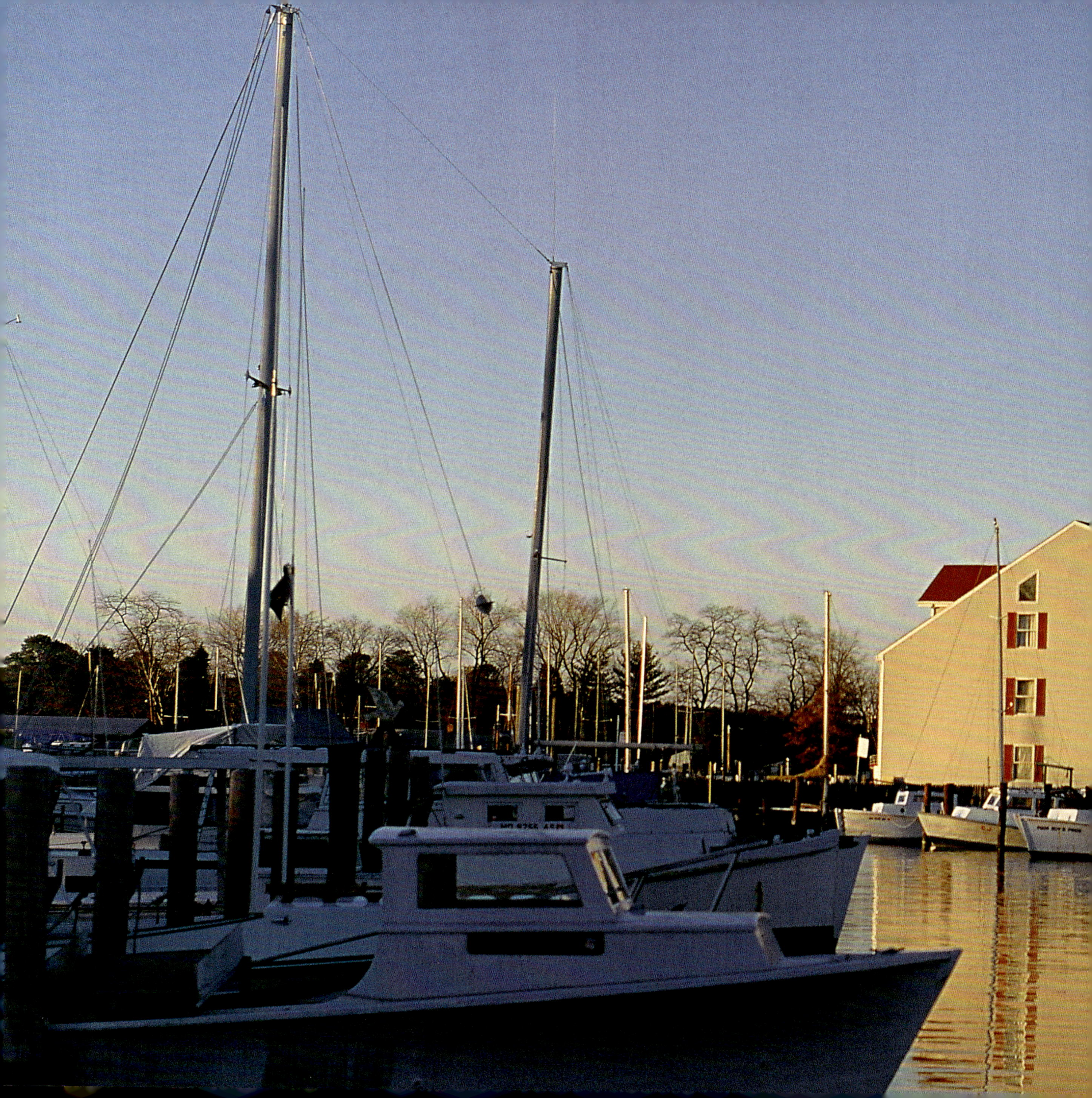

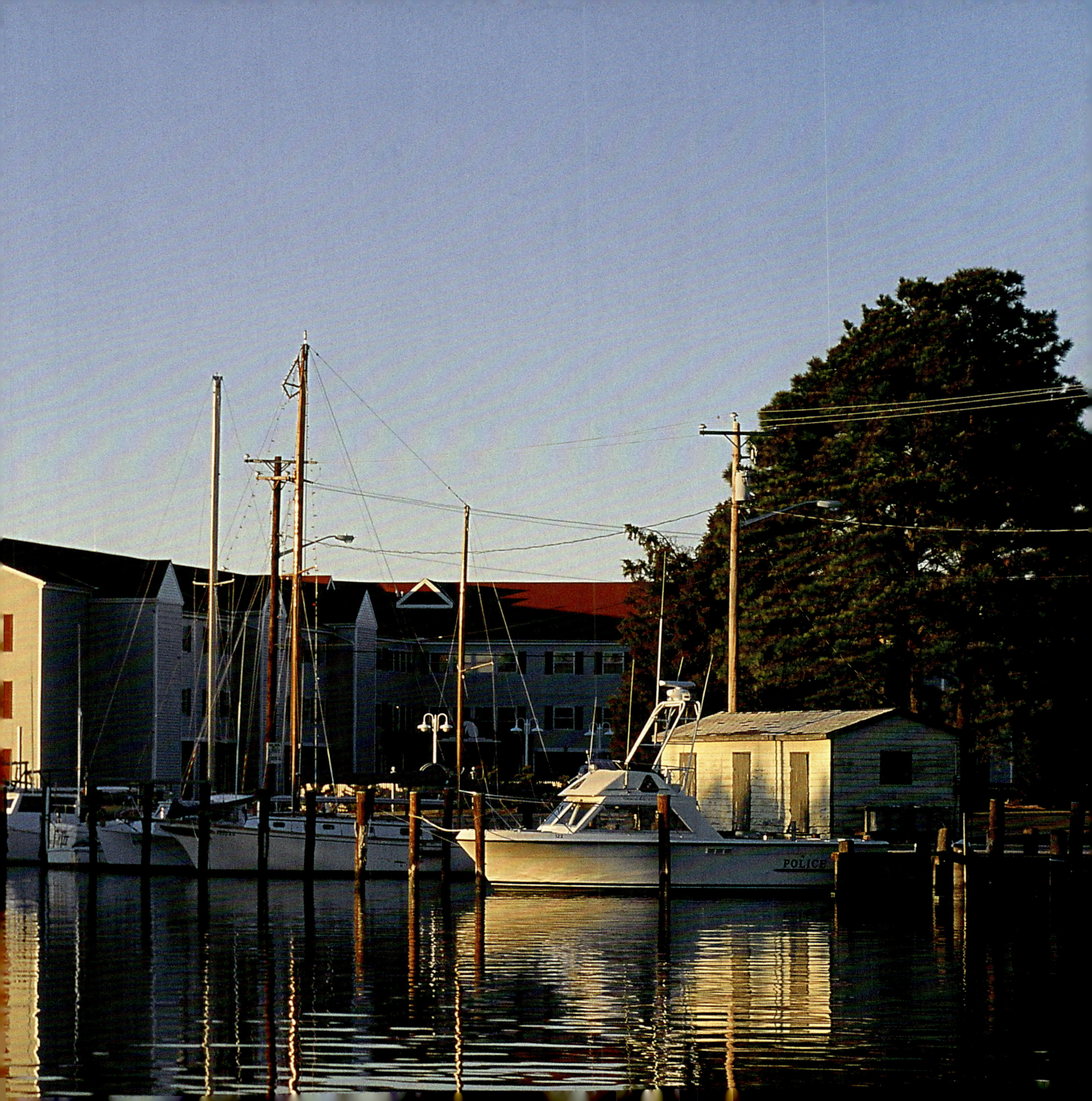
POLICE

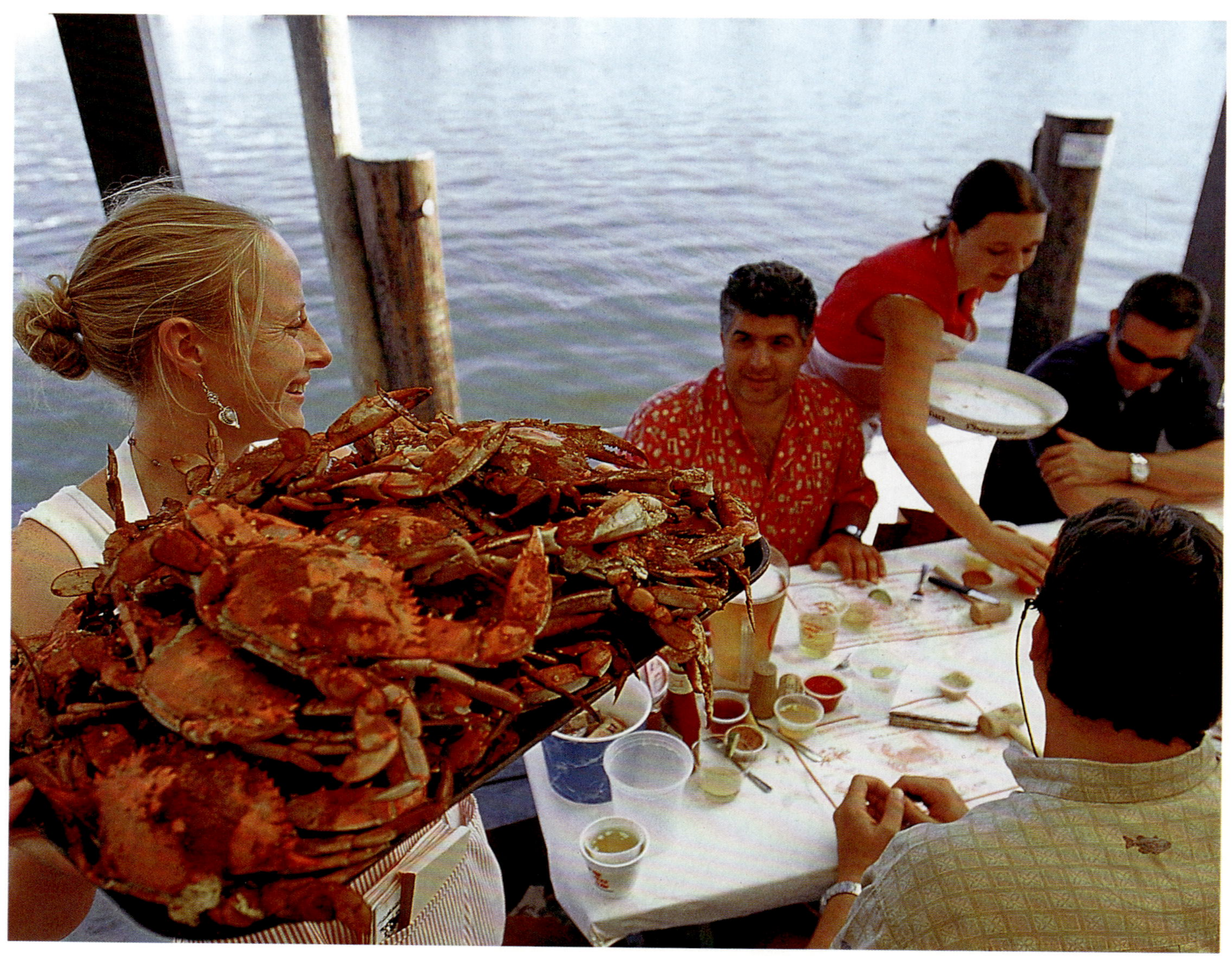

Diners enjoy a feast of blue crab, freshly caught in Chesapeake Bay. From crab cakes and crab balls to crab soup and crab sandwiches, there's no mistaking the specialty of the St. Michaels seafood restaurants.

Easton was founded in 1711 with the construction of the Talbot County Courthouse. Now home to 10,000 people, the community continues to serve as a commercial center for the surrounding seaside villages. Along with the courthouse, Easton's sites include a 1921 vaudeville theater and the Third Haven Friends Meeting House, one of the oldest places of worship in the nation.

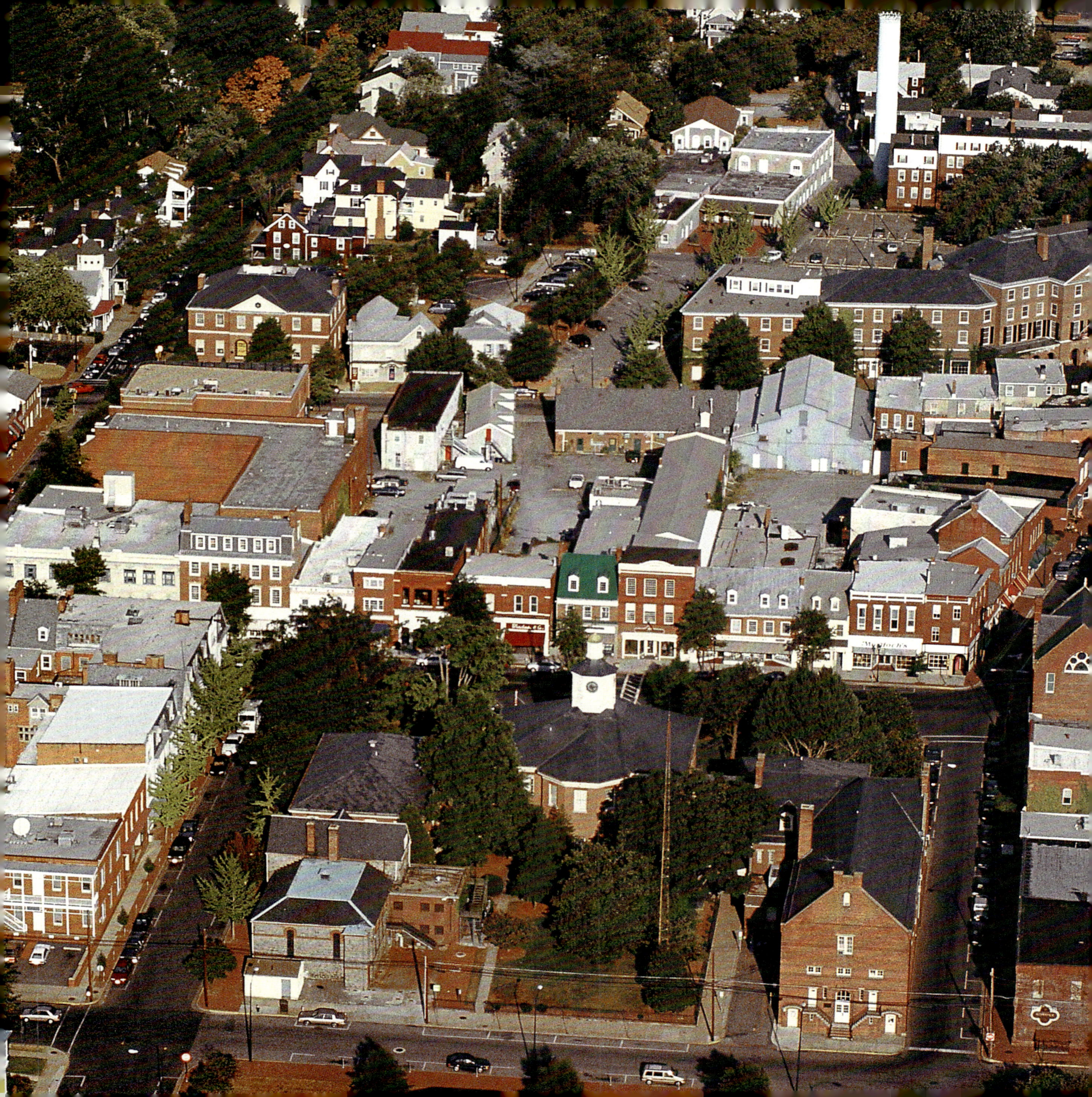

More than 65,000 people each year take part in 300 visual and performing arts programs and events at the Academy Art Museum in Easton. Housed in a renovated 1820s schoolhouse, the museum includes five galleries, dance studios, conference rooms, and a library.

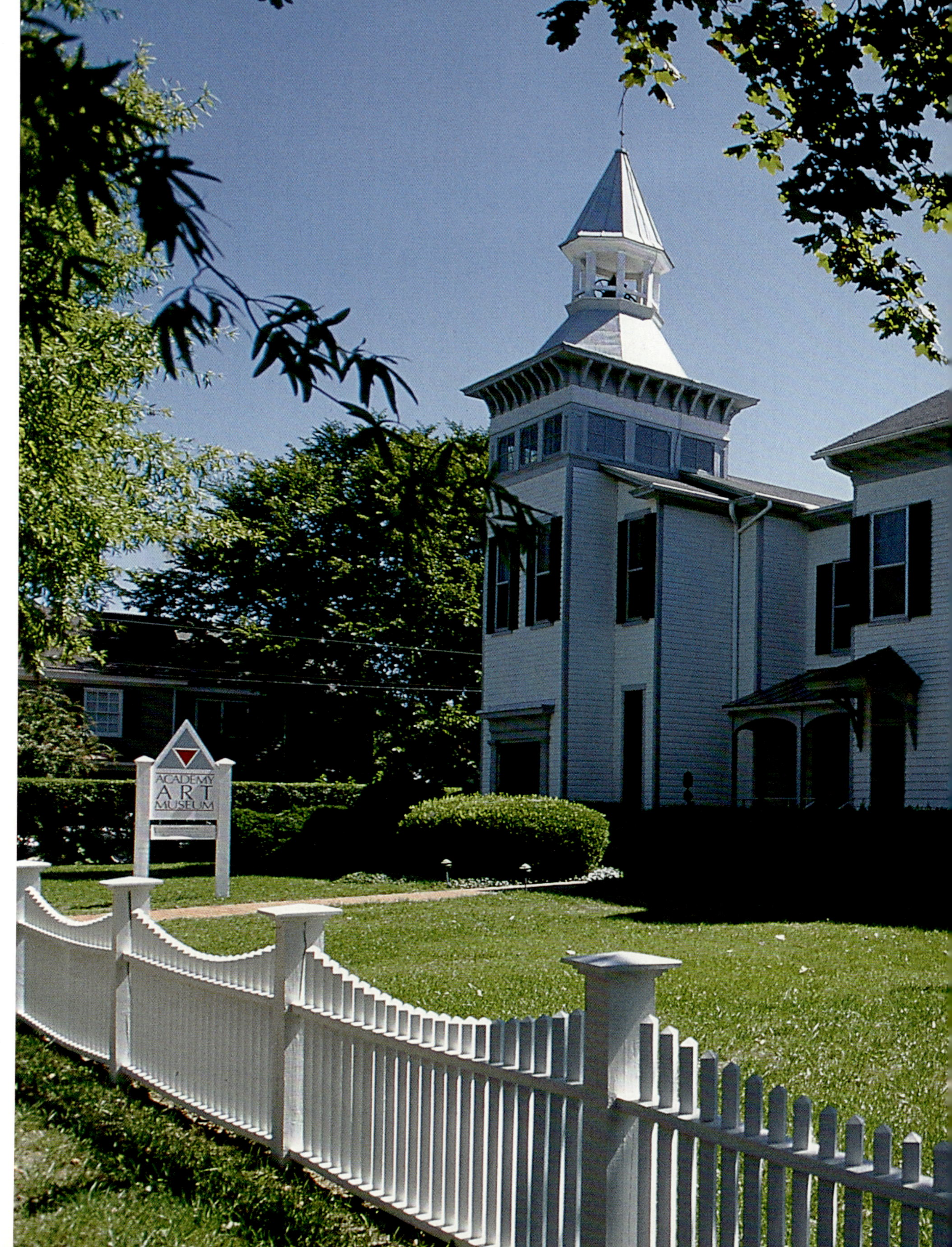

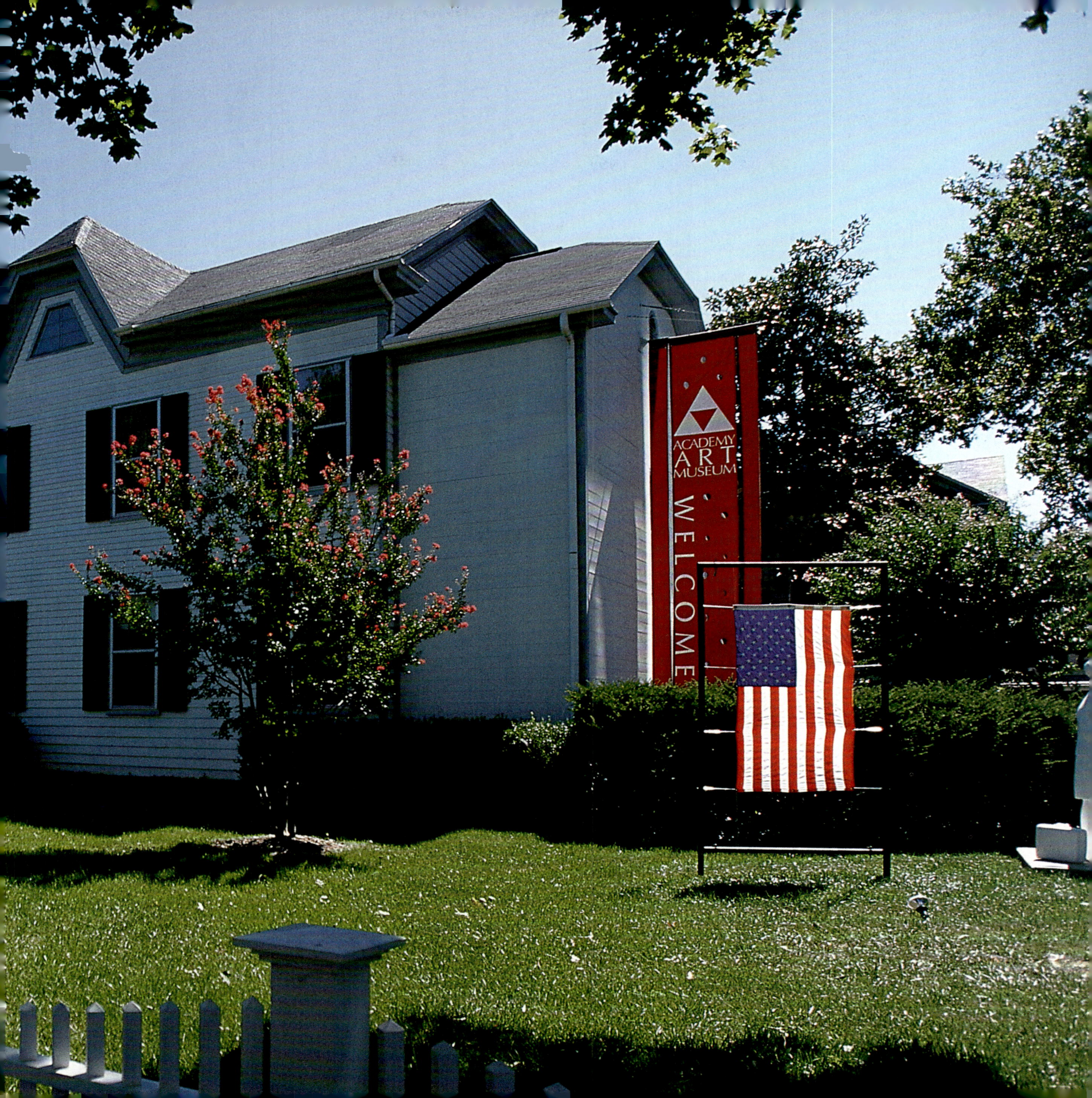
ACADEMY
ART
MUSEUM
WELCOME

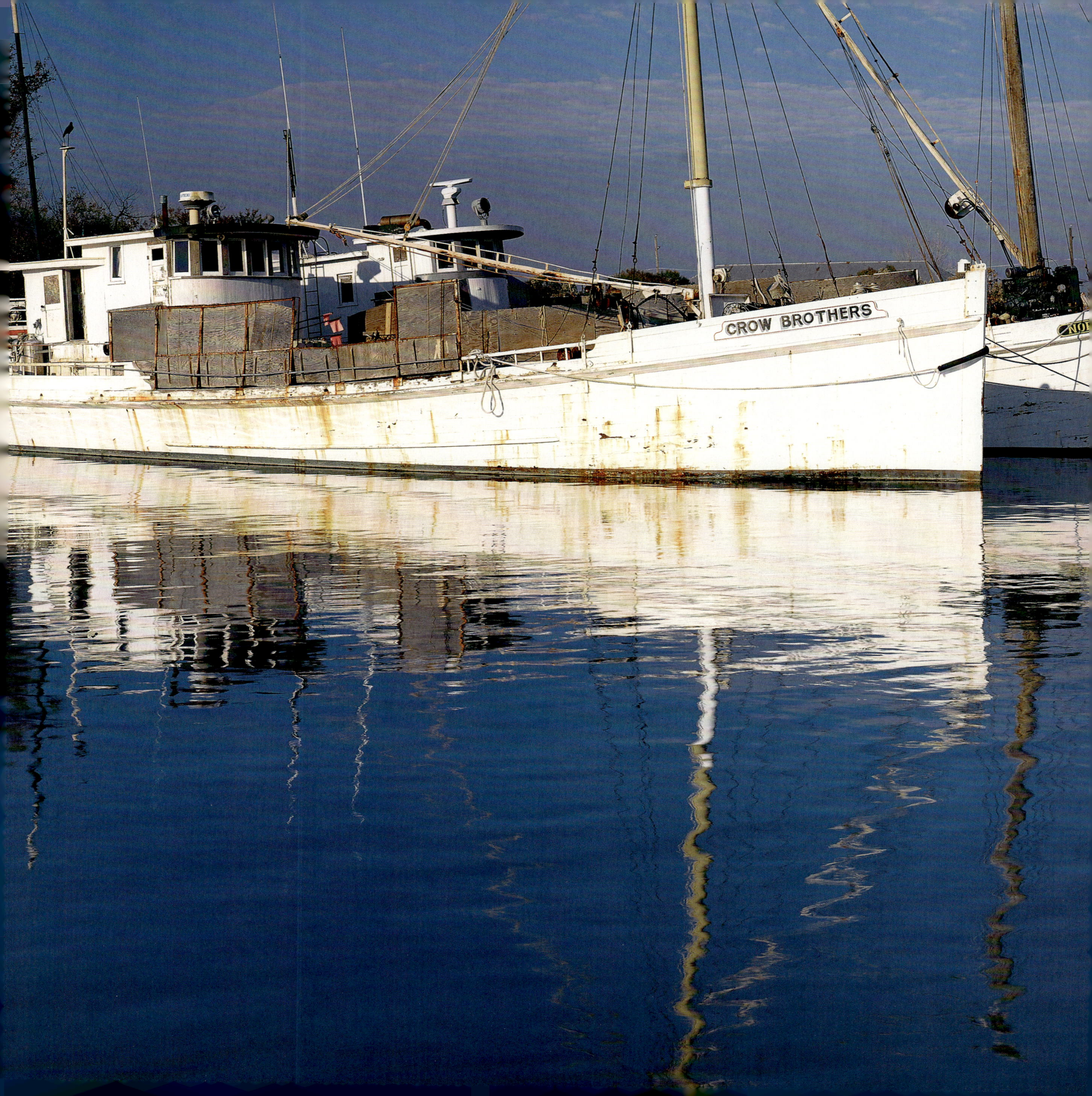
CROW BROTHERS

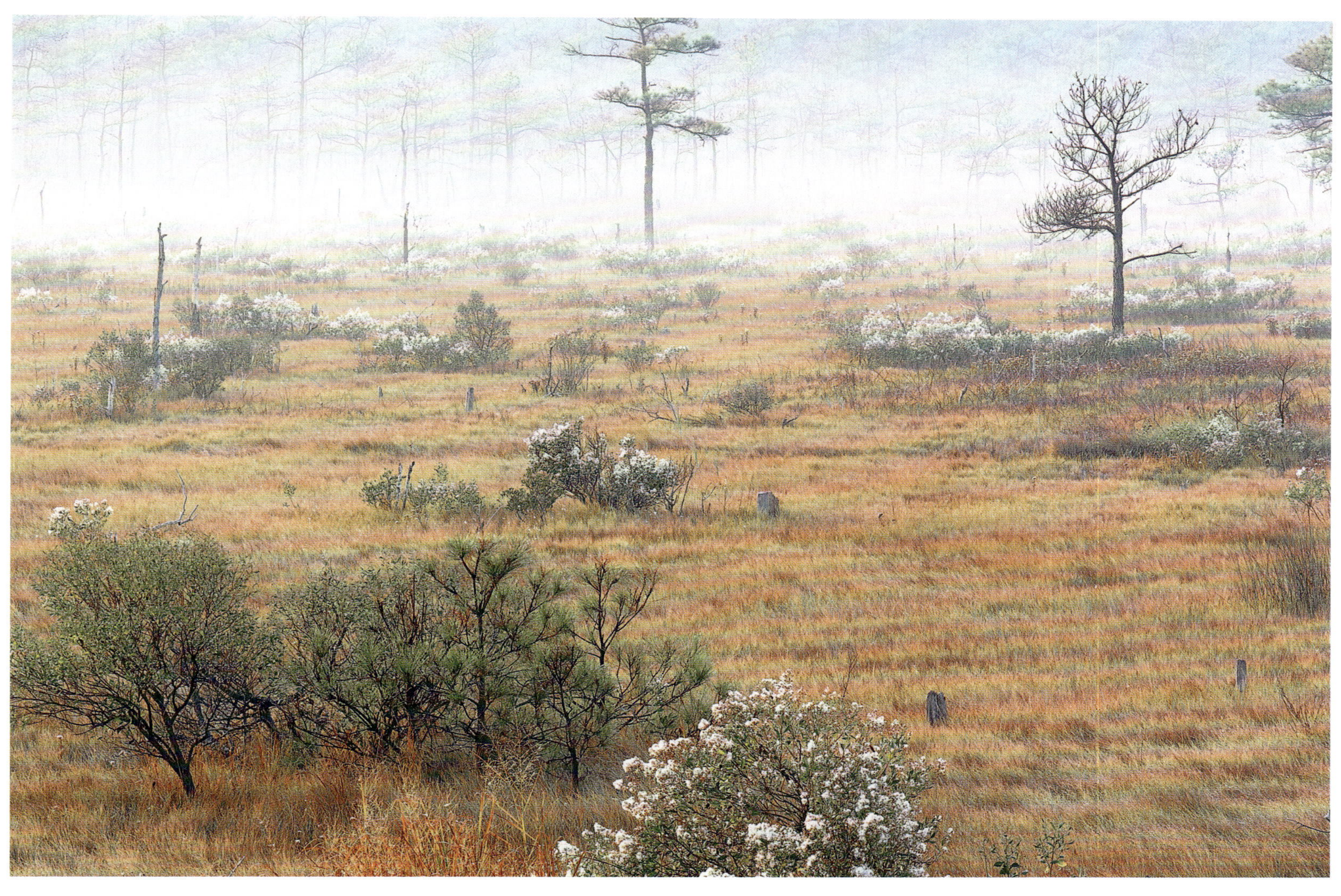

Freshwater tributaries and expansive salt marshes attract both paddlers and wildlife to Dorchester County. The wetlands offer refuge and plentiful food to bald eagles, ospreys, and endangered peregrine falcons as well as wintering tundra swans, Canada geese, snow geese, and more than 20 duck species.

Tilghman Island boasts a history as changeable as its name. Called Great Choptank Island, Foster's Island, Ward's Island, and finally Tilghman Island after a family of local residents, the region has been used for crops, raising livestock, and oyster harvesting. Bed and breakfasts, restaurants, and marinas now cater to vacationers.

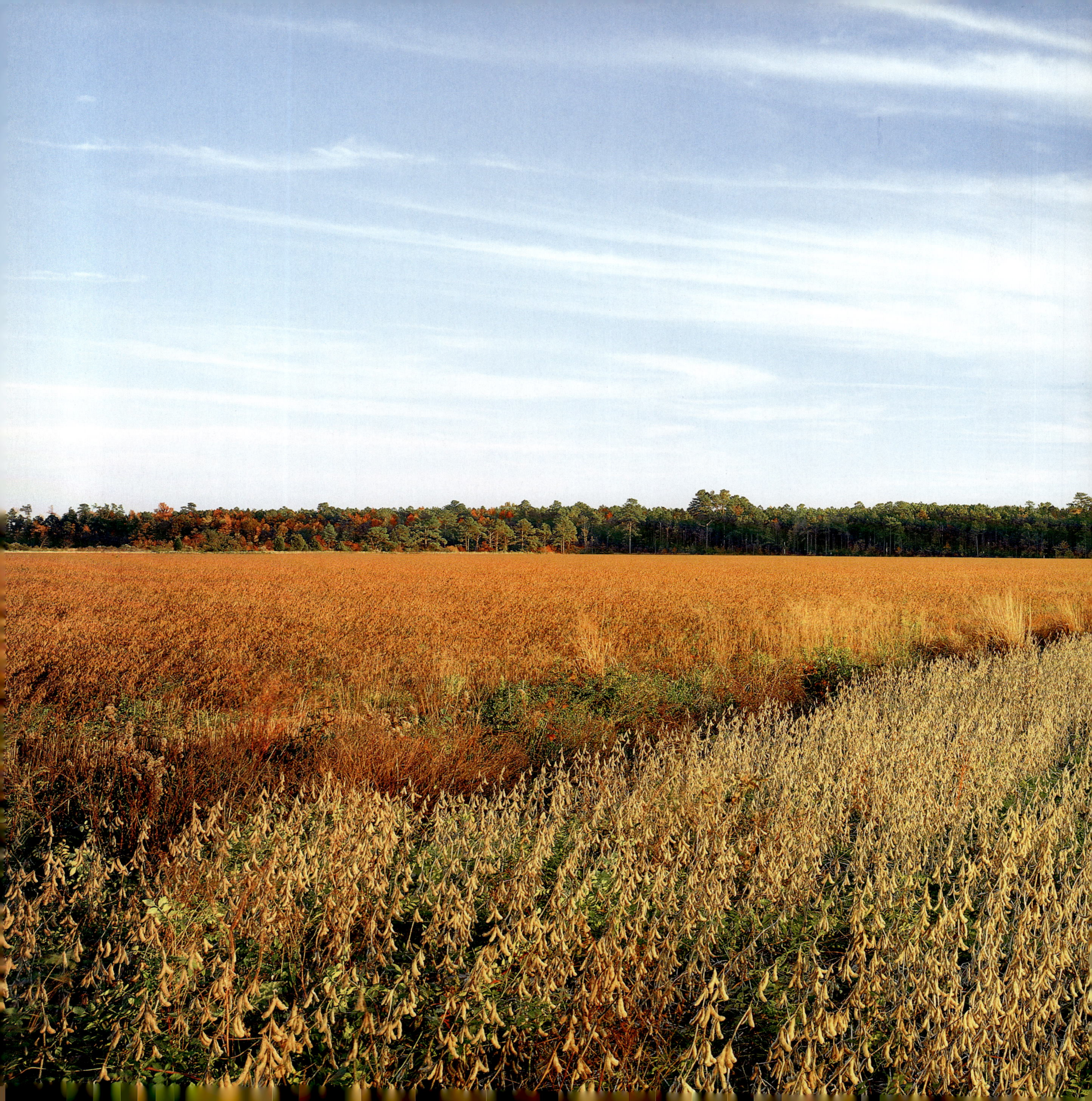

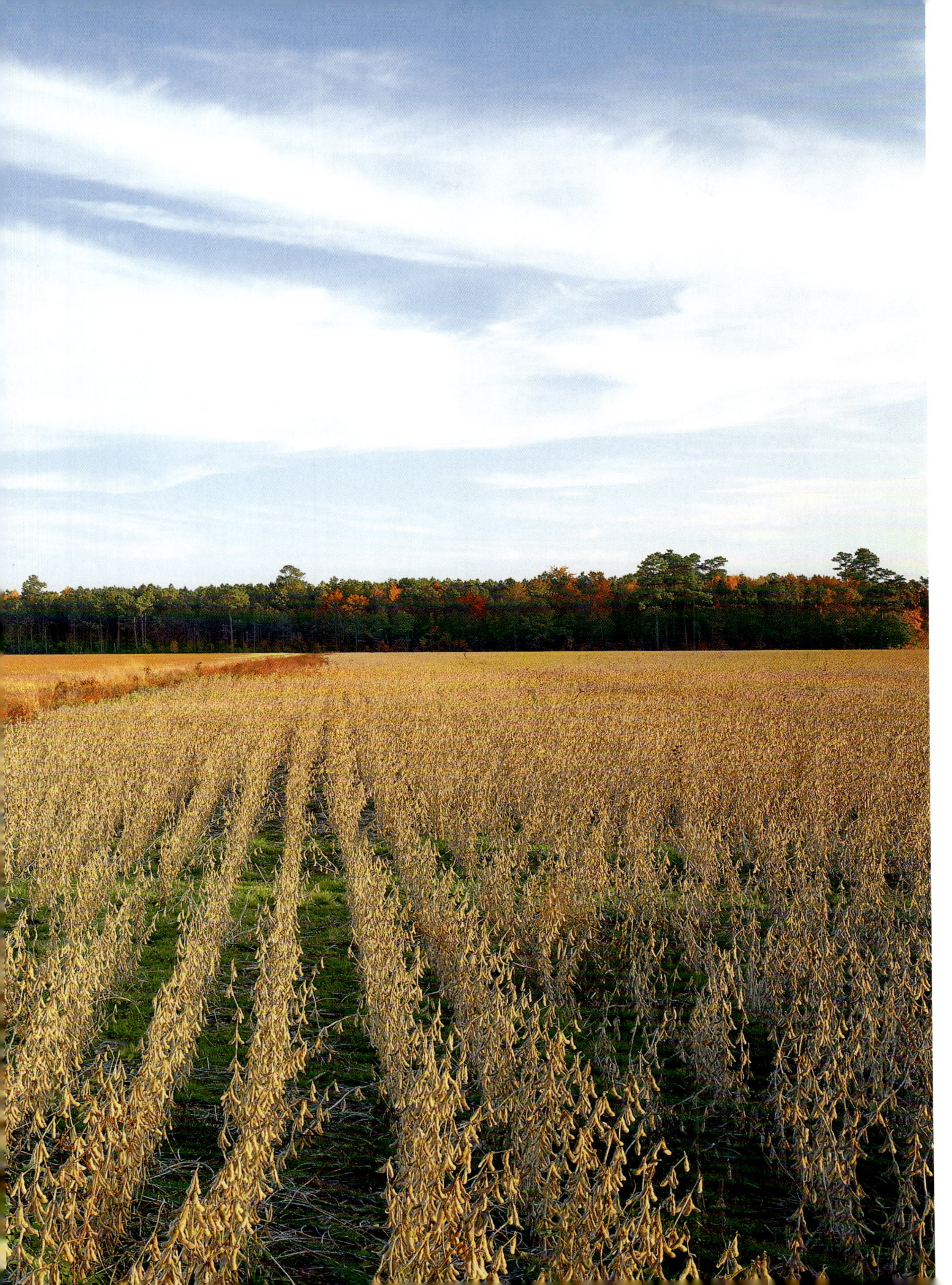

Soybeans are Dorchester County's second-largest crop, after corn. Although the region is best known for its shorelines and marshes—only about 20 miles of the county is bordered by land—about one-third of the area is used for agriculture.

In Smith Island's tiny fishing villages—Ewell, Rhodes Point, and Tylerton—residents have braved winter weather and rough seas for centuries, living a life so isolated that many speak with a distinctive accent. The island is named for Captain John Smith, who sailed Chesapeake Bay in 1608.

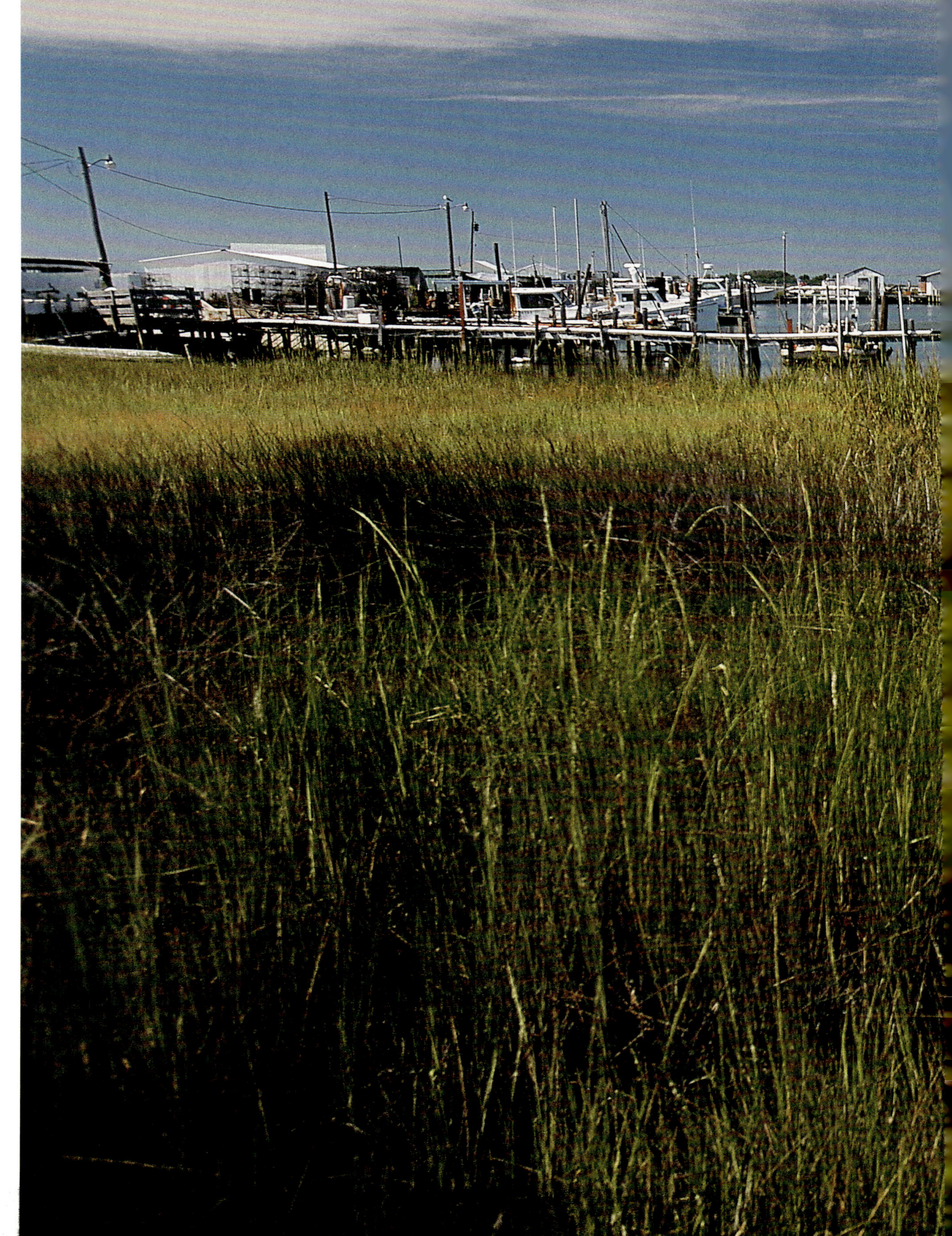

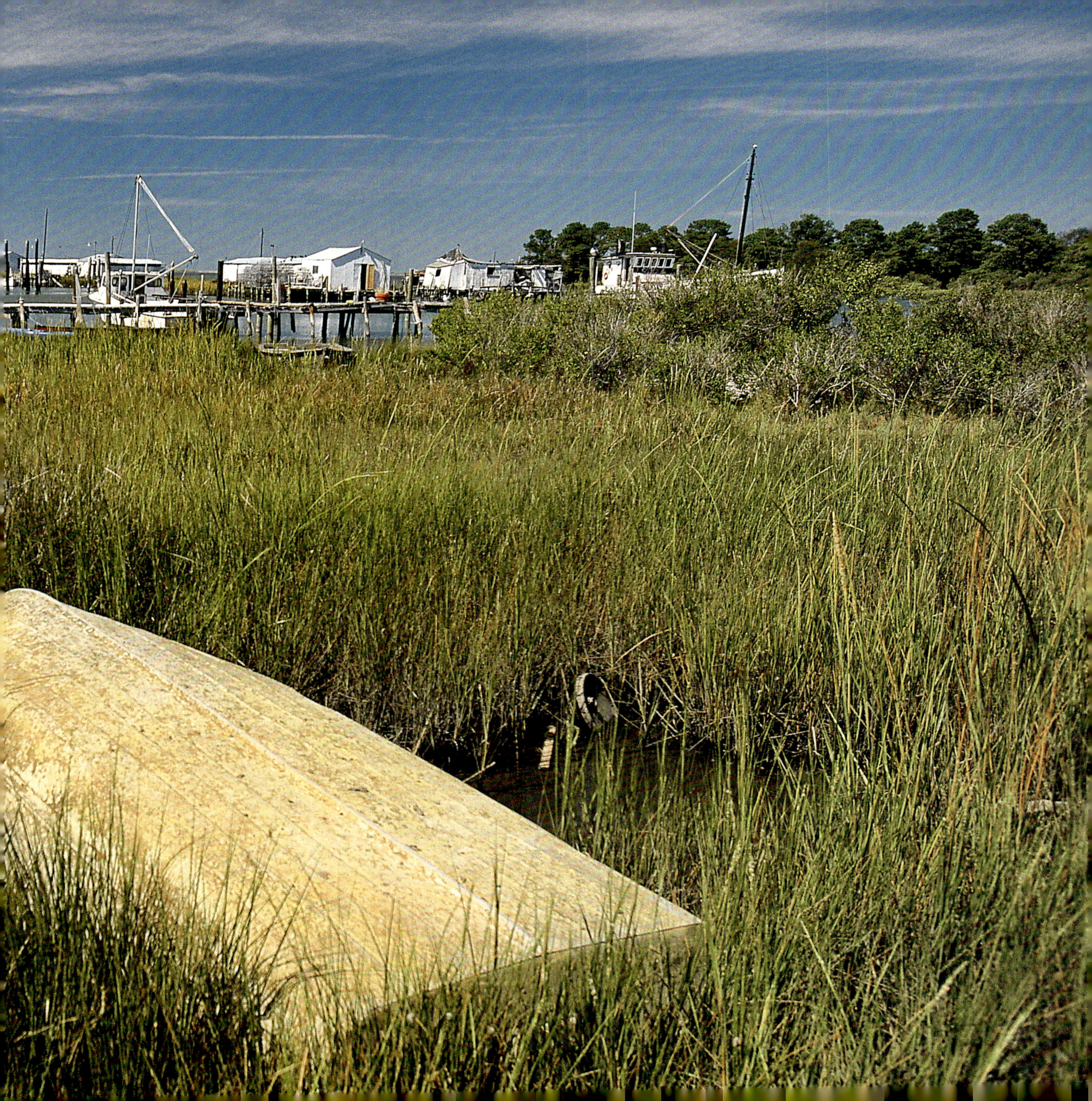

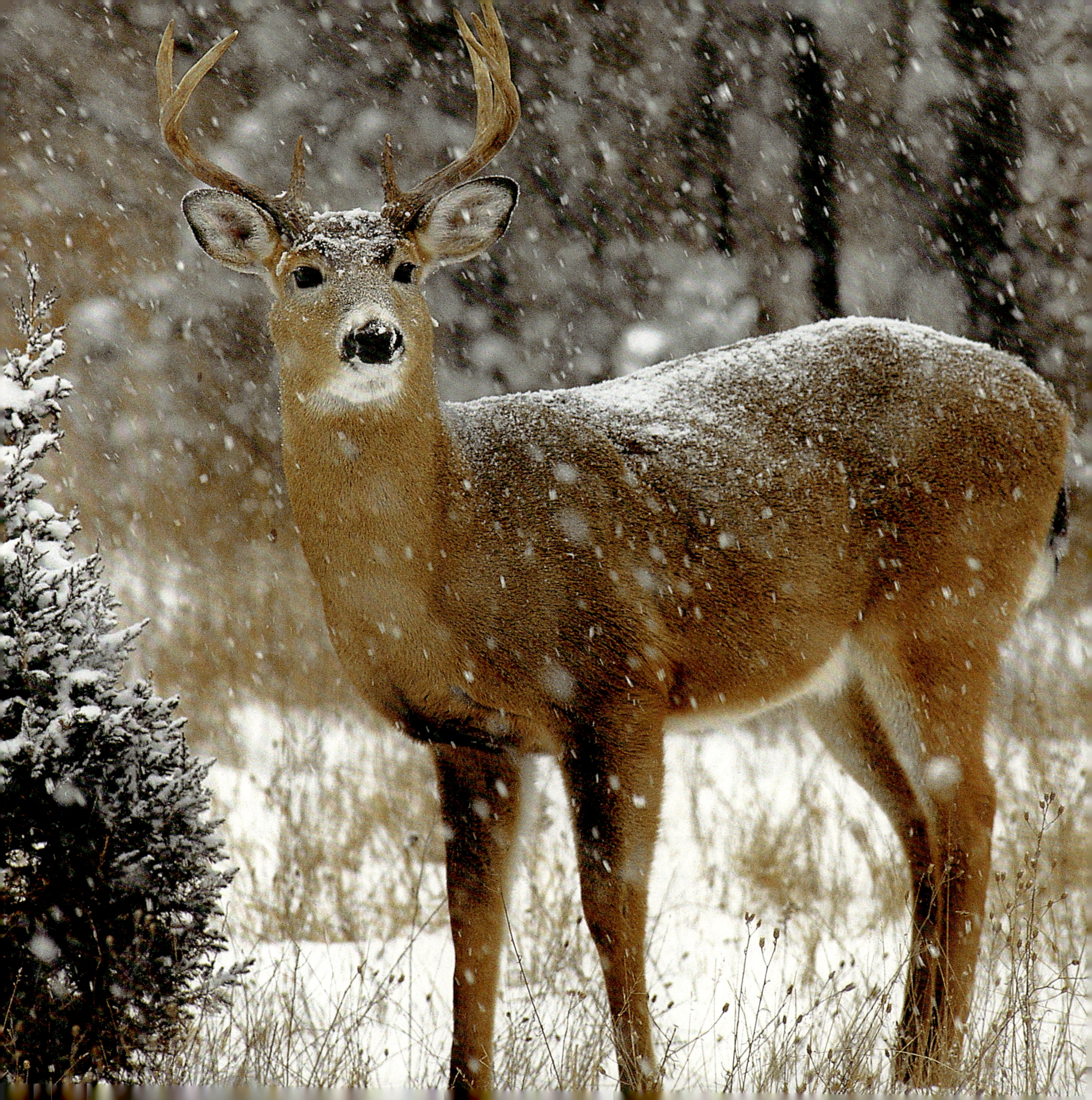

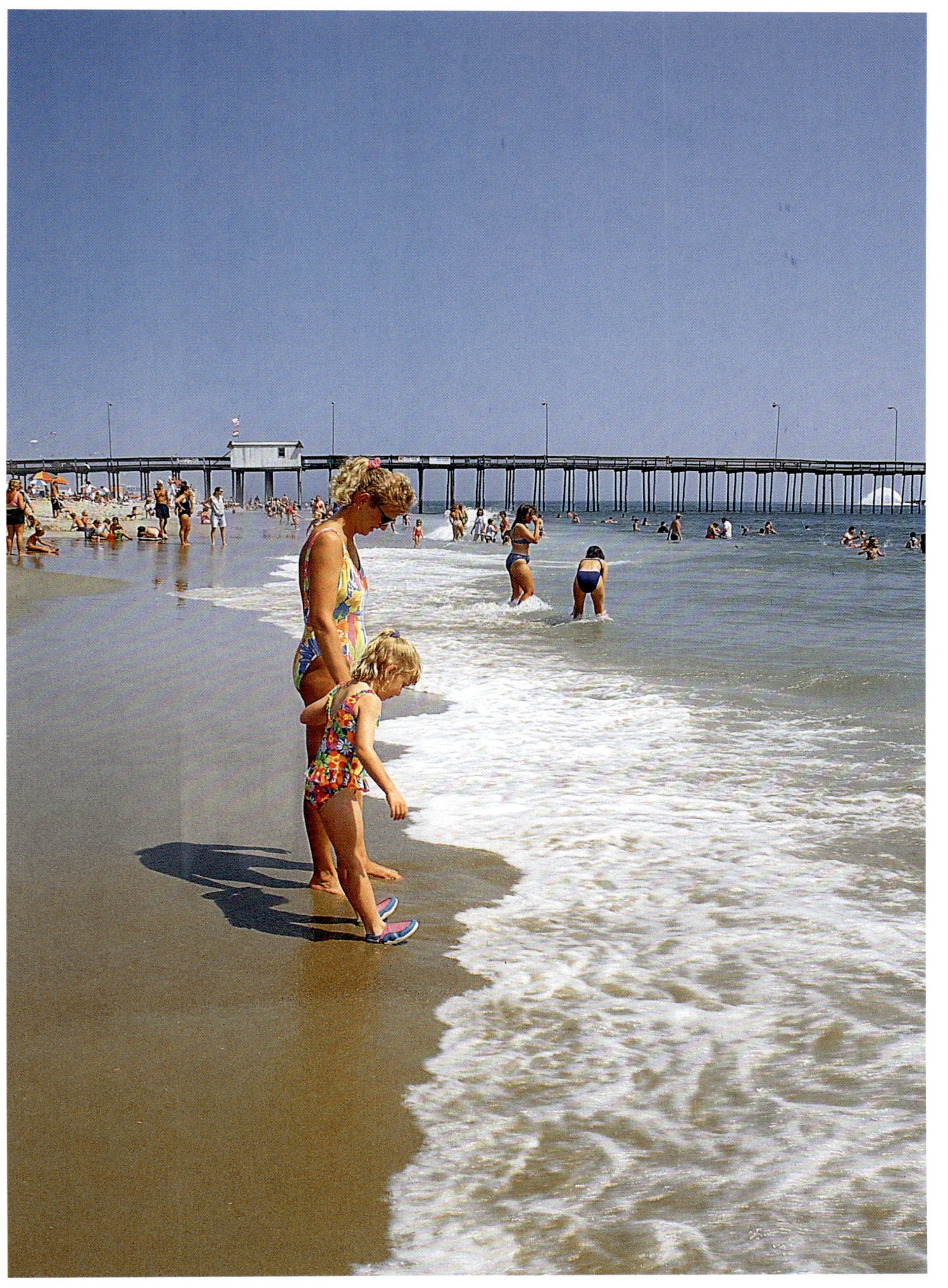

Seventeen golf courses, deep-sea fishing, nature preserve tours, water sports, and, of course, 10 miles of white sand beaches—these are the attractions of Ocean City, Maryland's most popular seaside resort city. More than 10,000 hotel rooms and 25,000 condominiums accommodate the sunseekers who arrive each summer.

Facing Page
Whitetail deer roam the woodlands of Pocomoke River State Forest, a 14,753-acre preserve in Worcester County. The name Pocomoke means "black water," a reference to the dark channels of the waterway, which winds for 45 miles from the Great Cypress Swamp in Delaware to the shores of Chesapeake Bay.

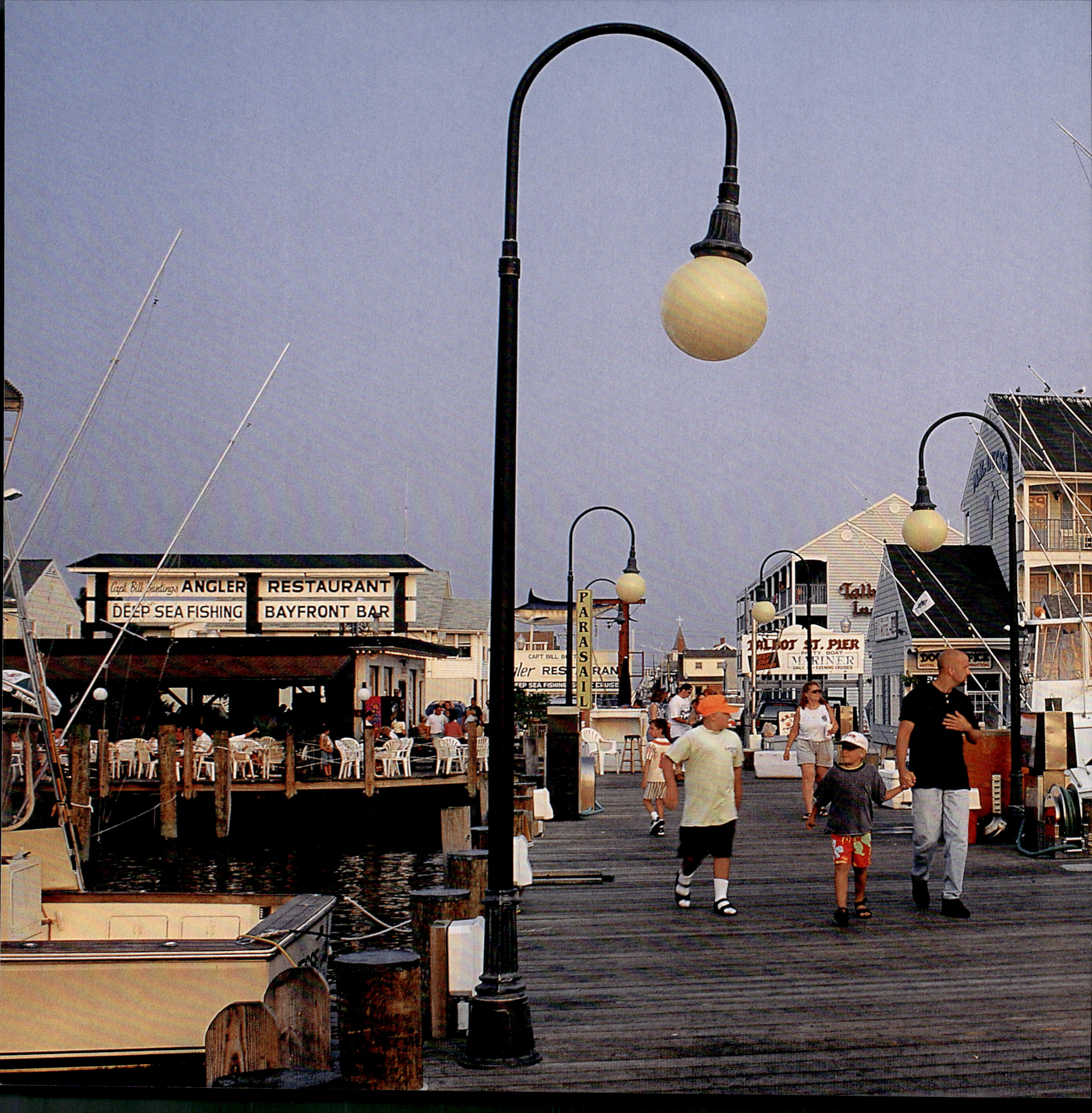

Capt. Bill Bunting's ANGLER RESTAURANT
DEEP SEA FISHING BAYFRONT BAR
PARASAIL
TALBOT ST. PIER
MARINER

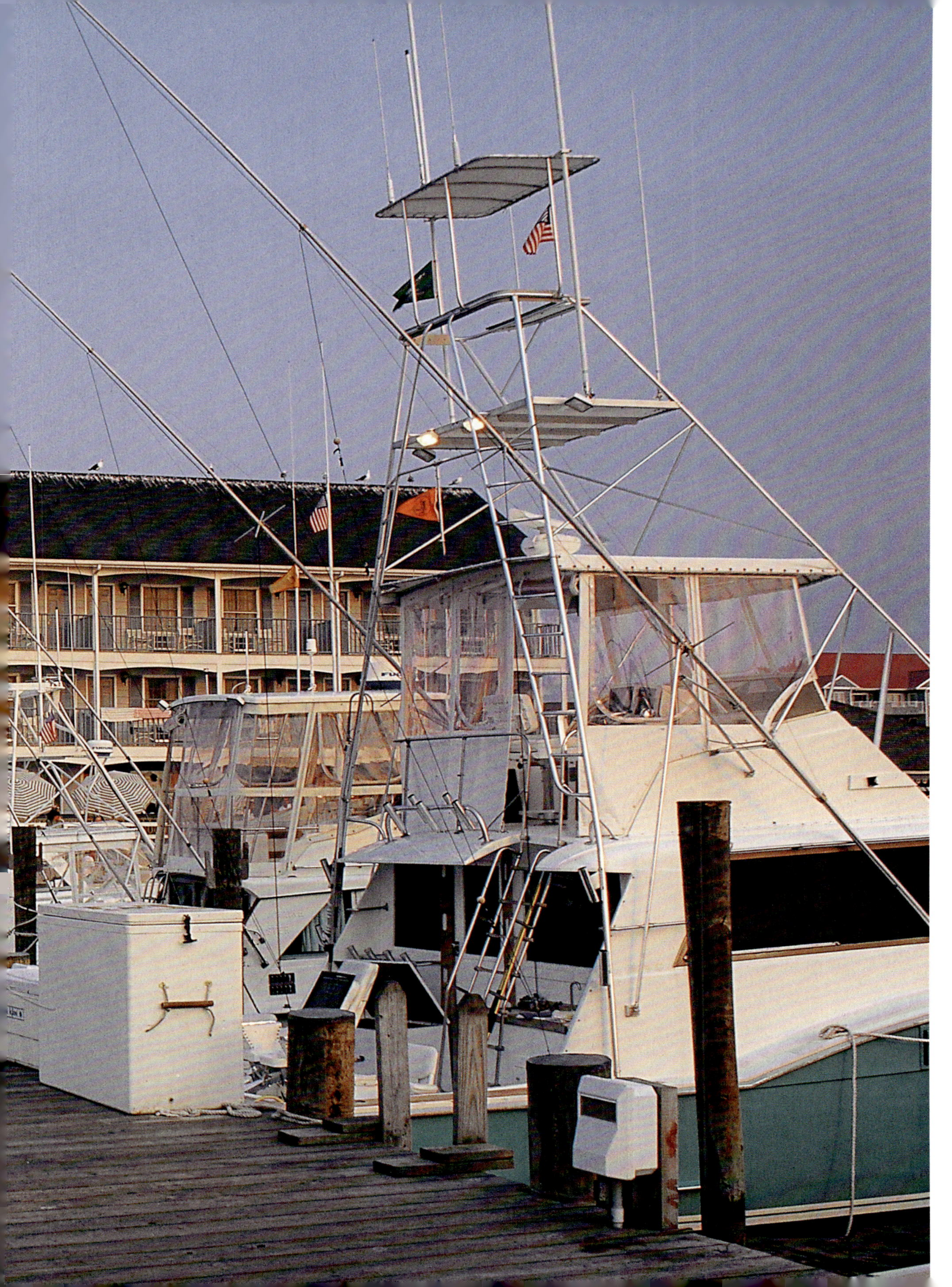

At the Talbot Street Pier in Ocean City, sport fishers proudly display their catches, tour boats depart for nearby Assateague Island, and shops offer bait, tackle, and advice. Ocean City has been luring vacationers since Isaac Coffin built the first guest cottage here in 1869.

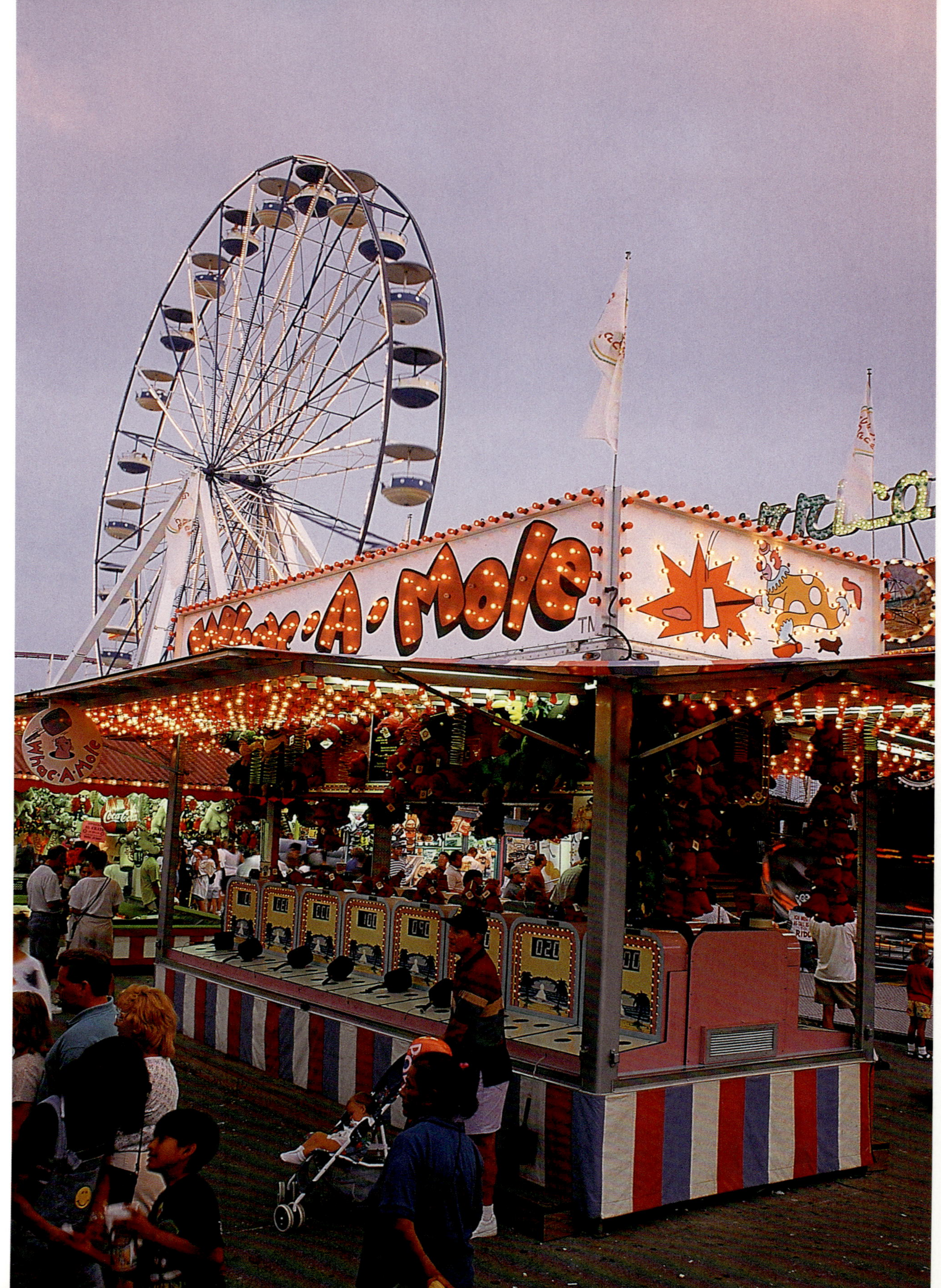

Ocean City's three-mile-long boardwalk offers countless entertainment options, from amusement park rides and arcades to saltwater taffy vendors and gift shops. A boardwalk train runs alongside the promenade throughout the summer.

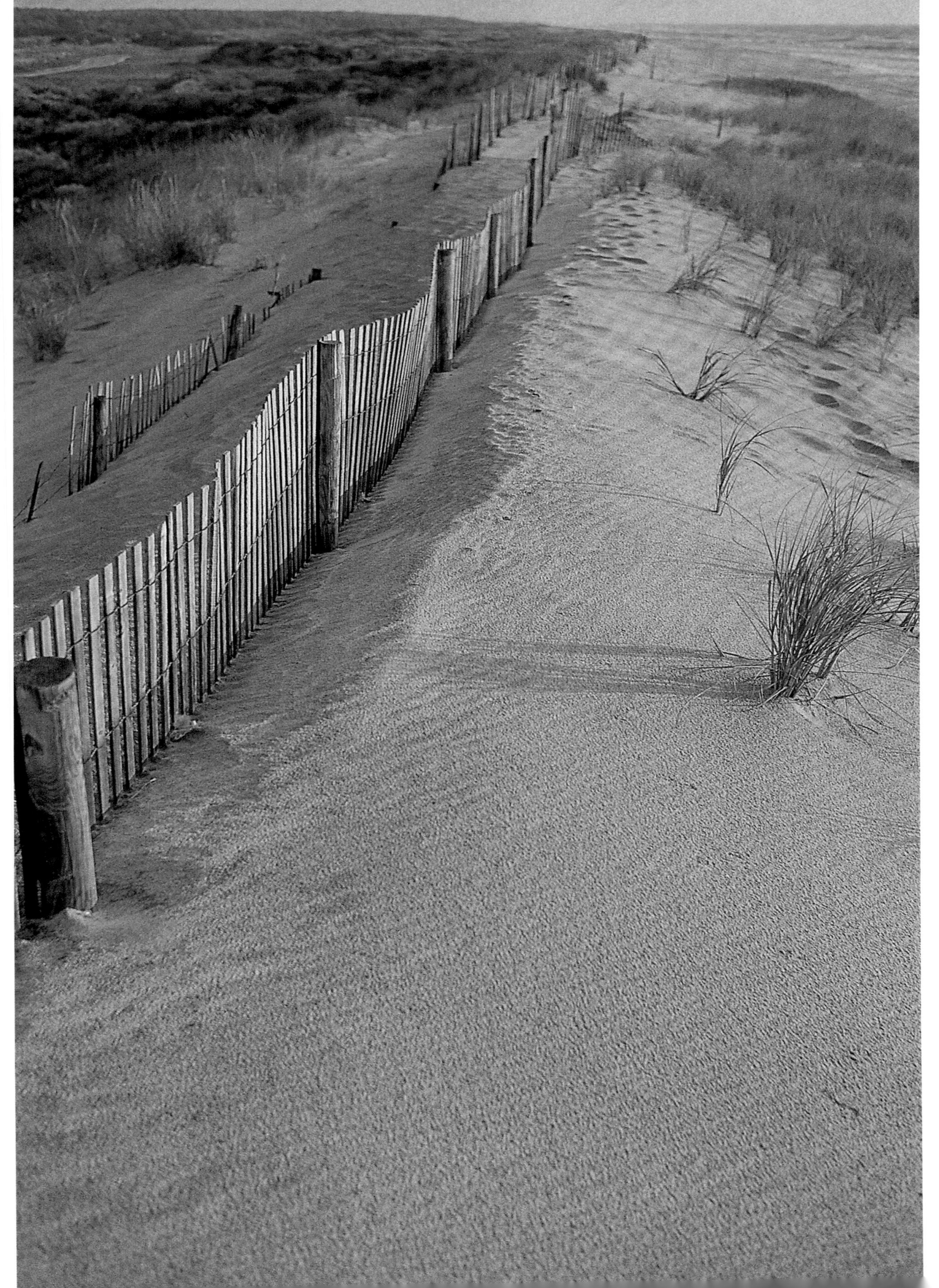

Lined with small cottages, the sands of Assateague Island were once connected to Ocean City. A 1933 hurricane separated the island and another storm in 1962 destroyed many of the local homes and streets. The island became a national seashore in 1965.

Assateague Island National Seashore protects the 37-mile-long island, home to wild ponies and more than 300 bird species. As the waves of the Atlantic constantly batter the barrier island, the sands slowly move. Historic maps show that the preserve has shifted a quarter-mile further inland since 1866.

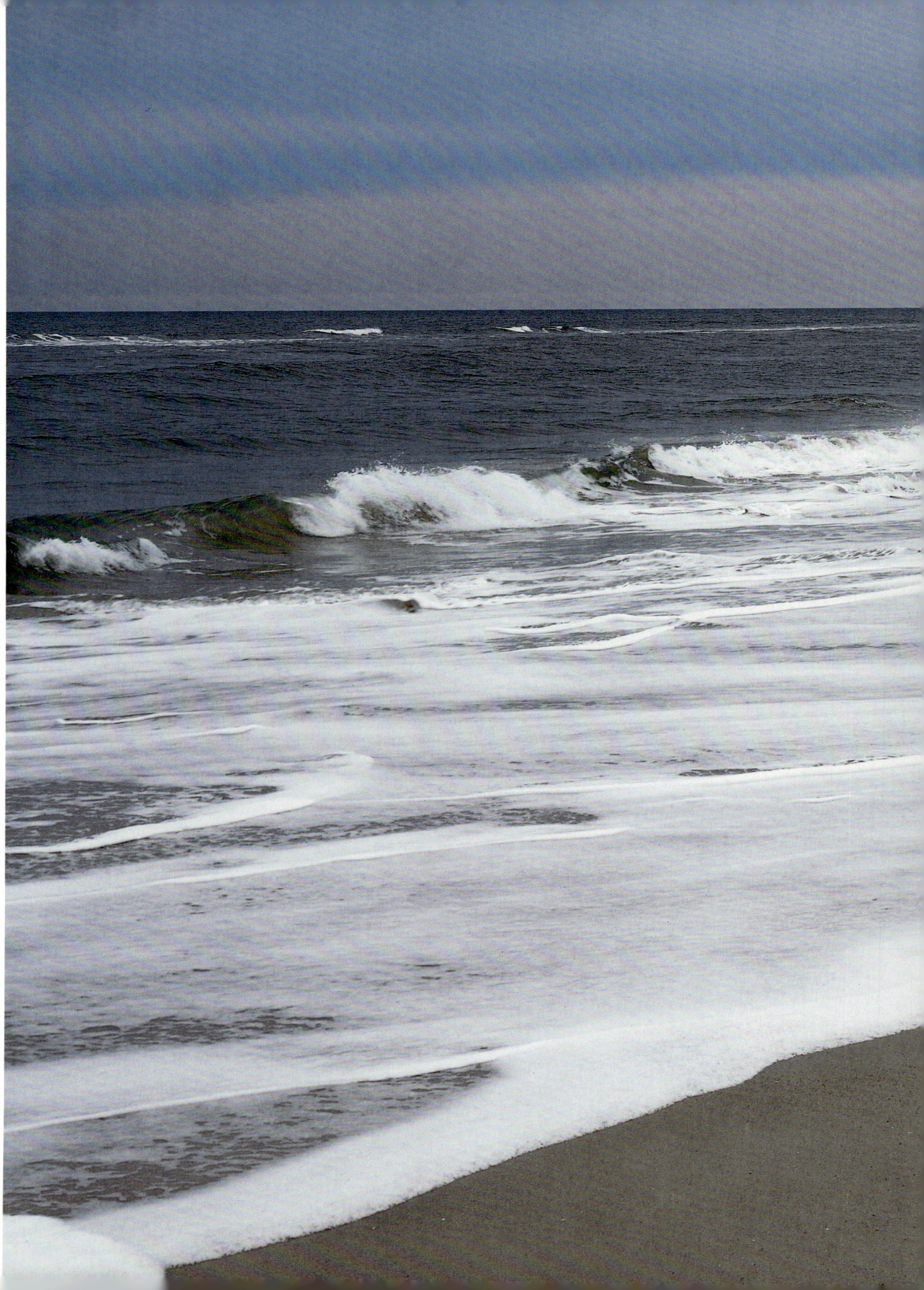

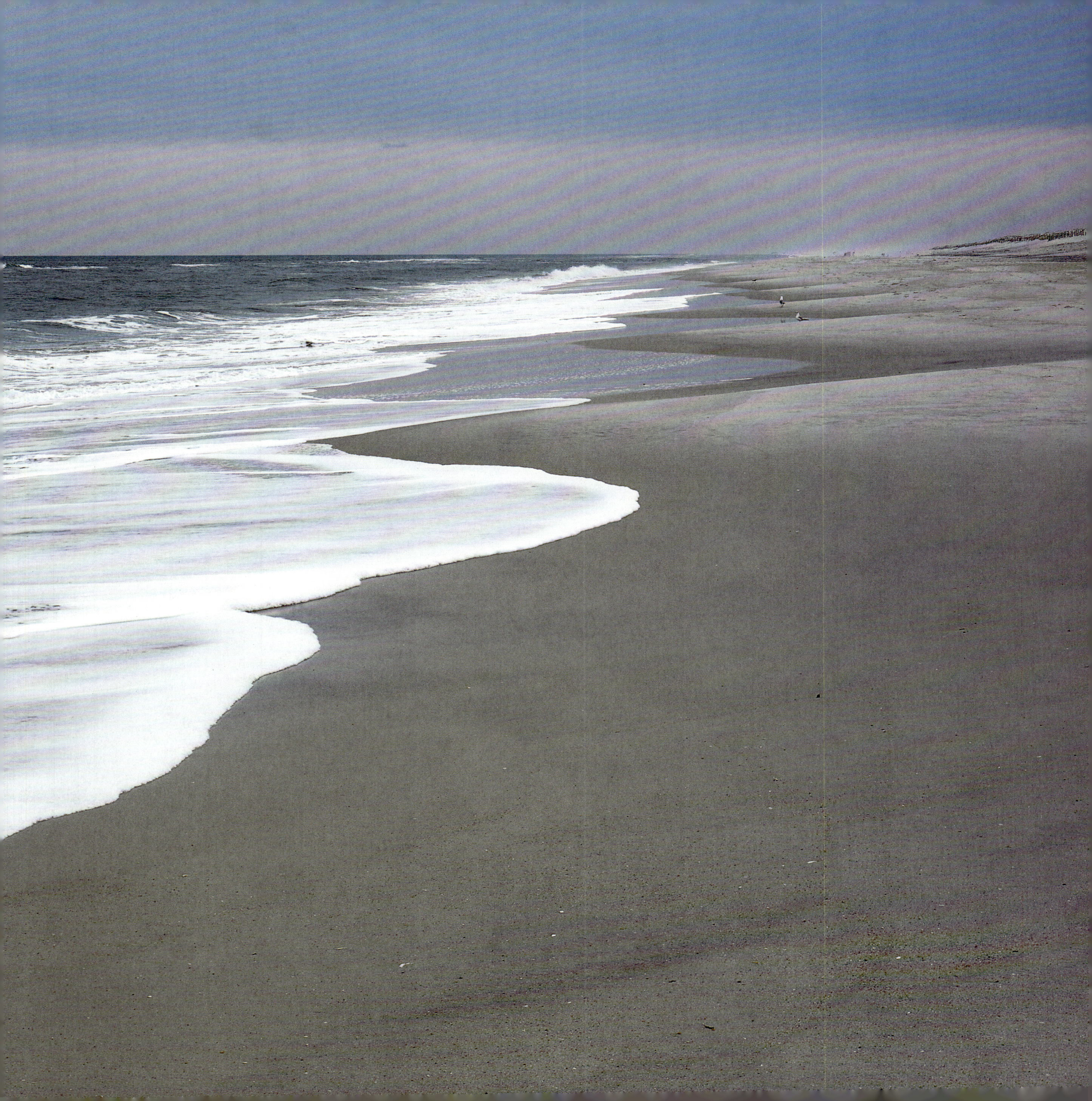

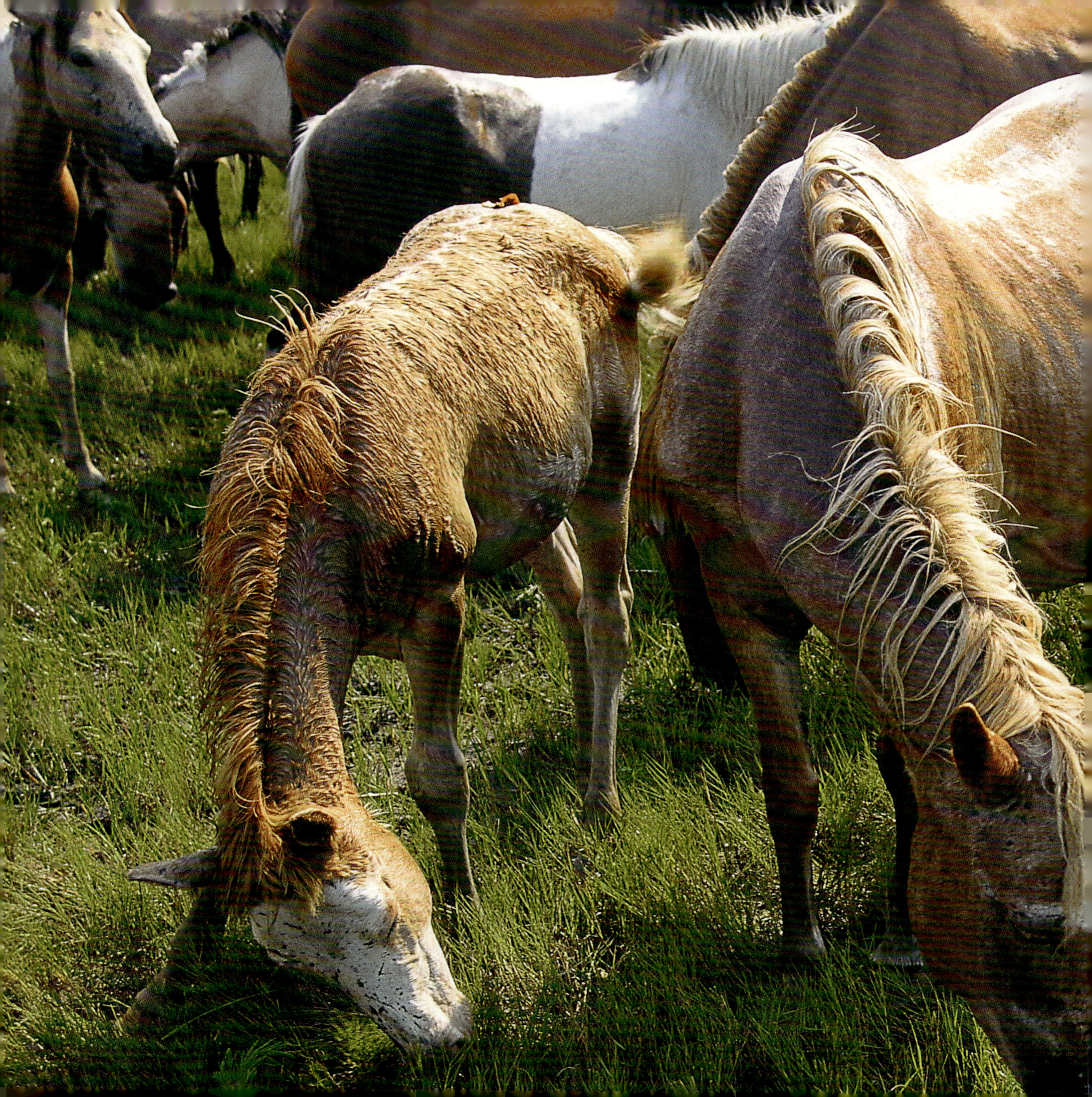

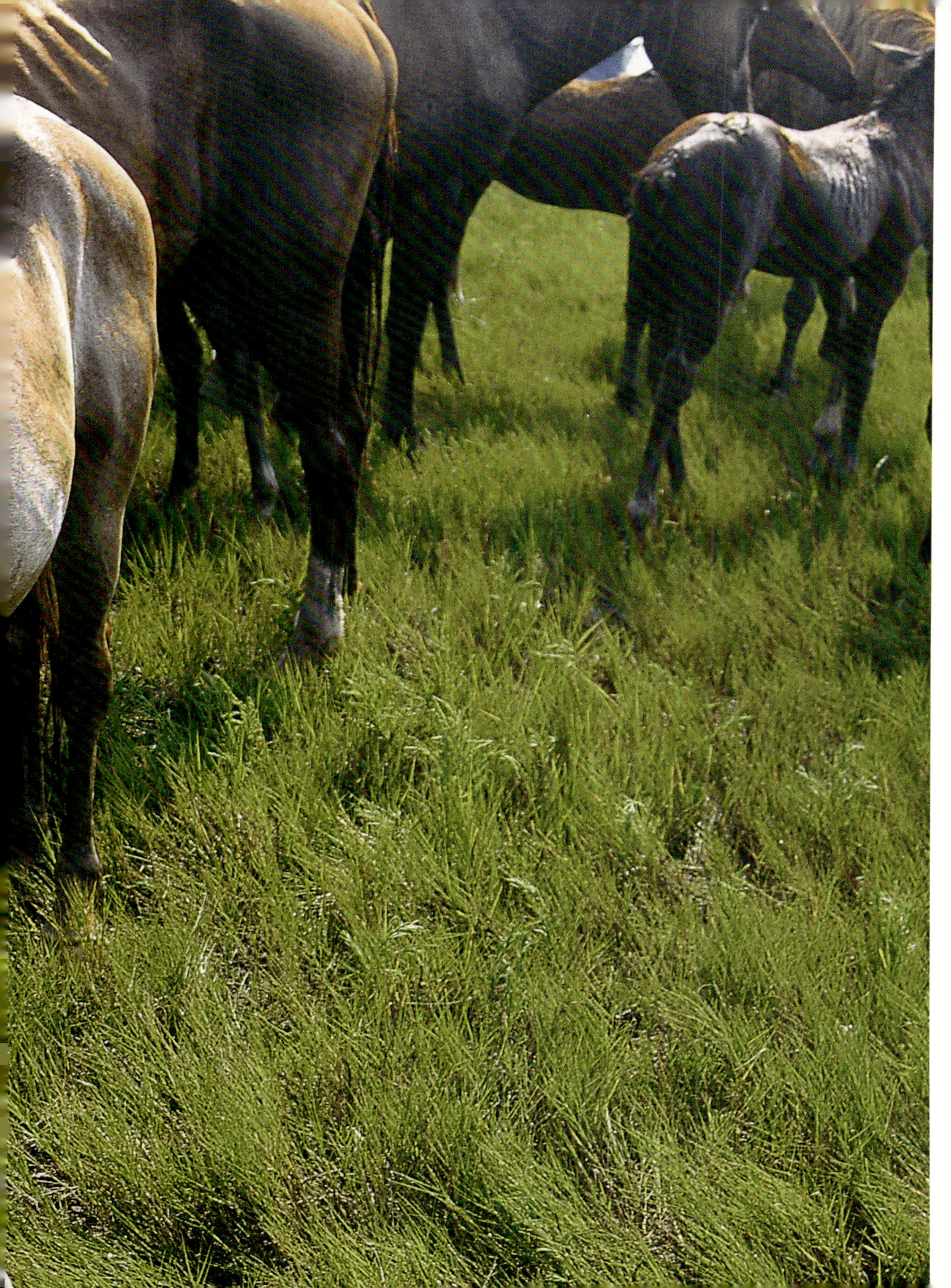

Many locals maintain that the wild ponies of Assateague Island are descended from horses that swam ashore from a shipwrecked Spanish galleon. However, park officials believe the horses were more likely brought to the island by seventeenth-century mainland farmers trying to avoid their taxes.

Photo Credits

Walter Bibikow/Folio, Inc 1, 3

Michael Ventura 6–7, 8, 9, 10–11, 12, 13, 15, 16–17, 24–25, 31, 34, 37, 43, 44, 46–47, 48–49, 50, 56, 60, 61, 62–63, 64, 69, 72–73, 76, 78–79, 84–85

Tom Till 14, 18, 19, 20–21, 42, 45

Peter Souza/Folio, Inc. 22

John Skowronski/Folio, Inc. 23, 68

Richard T. Nowitz/Photri, Inc. 26, 32–33

Richard T. Nowitz/Folio, Inc. 27, 28–29, 40, 54, 66

Richard Cummins/Folio, Inc. 30

Bill Kreykenbohm/Photri, Inc. 35

Mark E. Gibson/Dembinsky Photo Assoc 36, 41

Middleton Evans/Folio, Inc. 38–39

Richard Cummins/Folio, Inc. 51, 55

Vladpans/Folio, Inc. 52, 57

Bruce Leighton/Photri, Inc. 53

Llewellyn/Folio, Inc. 58–59

Mark E. Gibson/Photri, Inc. 65

Paul Rezendes 67, 70, 71, 80, 81, 82–83, 92–93

Harry Jordan/Mach 2 Stock Exchange 74–75, 77

Skip Moody/Dembinsky Photo Assoc 86

Mark E. Gibson/Folio, Inc. 87, 90

Mark E. Gibson/Unicorn Stock Photos 88–89

Michael Ventura/Folio, Inc. 91, 94–95